THE CLEOPATRA PAPERS

.... *A* ....

Private Correspondence

.... *By* ....

JACK BRODSKY and NATHAN WEISS

....

Simon and Schuster   New York

1963

Excerpts from this book
first appeared in *Esquire*

LIBRARY OF CONGRESS CATALOG CARD NUMBER: 63-19909

MANUFACTURED IN THE UNITED STATES OF AMERICA

BY H. WOLFF, NEW YORK

PREFACE

■■■■■■■■■■■■■

We always supposed that diaries were kept by teen-aged girls, and that memoirs were written by men in their seventies. What then were we doing in keeping the written record that constitutes this volume? We are not teen-aged girls, indeed we are not girls at all, and our median age is thirty-five, which is only half of seventy.

It probably began, as you shall see, in the charge that we—Weiss, the publicity manager of 20th Century-Fox Film Corporation, and Brodsky, the assistant publicity manager, both normally stationed at the company's home office in New York—were not performing our jobs adequately in that the film Cleopatra, on which the troubled company's future security greatly depended, was not getting enough publicity. This was told us repeatedly by top executives of the company during the first six weeks of the production that finally "took," the one that started in Rome on September 25, 1961, and essentially finished there on July 28, 1962—the time span covered in these pages.

From the very beginning, there was fear that Cleopatra would not be sufficiently publicized to insure that public anticipation would be so fervid as to return with a profit the cost of the original, abortive production in London as well as the one now starting in Rome. As has been recounted before, Cleopatra was in the planning stage for a number of years, and like any film during its period of preparation, inevitably devoured money without returning any to the company's treasury.

At last a production had started in London almost one year to the day before the production with which we are concerned. When it started over again in Rome a year later, the principal differences were that Richard Burton had replaced Stephen Boyd as Antony, Rex Harrison had supplanted Peter Finch as Caesar, and Joseph L. Mankiewicz had taken over as director (and chief writer) from Rouben Mamoulian. Cleopatra remained Elizabeth Taylor, and the producer, Walter Wanger: these were the constant elements from start to finish. By now, September of 1961, perhaps five million dollars had been expended on Cleopatra without anything yet on film that was to be used. By now, too, Fox had suffered reverses on box-office expectations held for a number of other films, and as a result there was strife within the internal management of the company which had begun to attract abnormal interest from the press, the stockholders and Wall Street brokerage houses.

The situation at Fox was not just a battle between two forces. The weakening of the authority of the president, Spyros P. Skouras, at the hands of new Wall Street groups was complicated by the emergence of a "third force" in an Old Guard within Fox that felt it could capitalize on the newly diluted strength of the once unassailable Skouras.

Undoubtedly the nerves of all concerned were under strain, otherwise how could it be fairly argued that Cleopatra was not receiving "enough publicity"? Apart from the interest in the subject, and the growing public knowledge of the company problems, there was Elizabeth Taylor. Over the Cleopatra years, and the ones immediately preceding them, she had become the unique celebrity of the film world, for all the reasons both right and wrong: her talent, her beauty, and her personal life. Most recently, she had been in public favor as the bereaved widow of Michael Todd; out of it when she and Eddie Fisher were married after Mr. Fisher and Debbie Reynolds, another actress, were divorced; in once again when an illness very nearly caused death during the year of non-production of Cleopatra in London. In to the point of winning the Academy Award as the best actress of 1960 for her performance in Butterfield 8.

One contention in mid-1961 was that perhaps the public was tired of Miss Taylor and Cleopatra, that the publicity peak on the film had been reached without the film even yet begun. True or not, Weiss, in Rome at the outset of the filming in late September and early October of 1961, appraised the situation as calling for special tactics. He therefore recommended, and it was quickly decided, that Brodsky should be deployed from his New York base to supervise the American publicity from the production site itself, while Weiss held down the publicity manager's office in New York by himself.

Brodsky arrived in Rome during the middle of October, and stayed at his post until late in April 1962. At that time his wife's difficult pregnancy forced their return to New York, and it was obvious that the solution that would best "protect" the interests of Cleopatra was for the two men to change places. Weiss and his wife therefore arrived in Rome on April 29, 1962, and stayed until the last day of production from that base, July 28, 1962. This volume of reportage is based upon the personal, out-of-office and after-hours correspondence between the two men throughout the original and later reversed assignments.

To return to the first question, what prompted it? All business relating to the film went into the regular, official business correspondence, none of which, of course, is reproduced here. But almost from the very start, extraordinary things began to happen, and friends had to communicate such information to each other quite separately from the conduct of business. The fact that each was now "alone" at his post, and not working side-by-side in New York as they had during several years of close friendship, probably contributed to the spontaneous development of an extensive private correspondence.

It should be said at the outset that were we to publish the whole body of correspondence, it would be very long and possibly very boring. By editing these letters, we have attempted to clarify and simplify, but never at the expense of truth. Also we have tried to avoid letters crossing except where necessary to present a truthful record, as the crossing of letters has been a confusion and annoyance to man from the time he started to write them. The phone conversations contained here are reconstructions.

It should be noted also that readers unfamiliar with show business—there may now be only a few of these, as Variety once sagely stated that it has become "everybody's other business"—may be startled by the casual, everyday use of what was once unprintable language. Within the film trade such language has by now become so conventional that, far from being vulgar, it can sound almost endearing, and no matter what man or woman speaks it within these pages, it never had the harsh ring in life it may still have for a few in print. For those few who do not want to be tested, there is still time to reconsider.

Finally, it probably is not giving away the ending to say that eventually Cleopatra did receive "enough publicity." To this day our friends wonder if we really played a part, or assuming that we did, what that part was, in fermenting the publicity on Cleopatra. To these friends who have urged us to "write a book" about our experiences; to our wives who, like twin Everests, were there through it all; particularly to our "guest writers" (not ghost) Dick Brooks, Greg Morrison and Larry Willig; and to Albert Da Silva, Byron Dobell, Bob Gottlieb and Ad Schulberg, each of whom knows the part he or she played, this book is dedicated.

JACK BRODSKY
NATHAN WEISS

New York, May 1963

viii

The Cast
of Principal Characters
■■■■■■■■■■■■■

■■■■■■■■■■■■■

ELIZABETH TAYLOR: While one might think that Miss Taylor needs
no introduction or number on her back, that the spectator can
identify this player with or without a scorecard, it is necessary to
pinpoint her role as a major participant in the *Papers*, for the
authors freely admit that without Miss Taylor there might have
been no *Papers*. The star was at first in the constant company
of her husband, Eddie Fisher, and then of Richard Burton. To
each she was remarkably faithful. To the authors she was alter-
nately the bane of their existence and the inspiration for the most
publicized film in motion-picture history. She is, of course, referred
to in these pages as Liz, Taylor, Miss Taylor and Elizabeth.

JOSEPH L. MANKIEWICZ: Writer-director of the film. Fiftyish, pipe-
smoking, seemingly never ruffled. He is also referred to in the
Papers as JLM, the Mank and simply as Joe. A multiple Academy
Award winner, his previous association with Miss Taylor (his
direction of her in *Suddenly, Last Summer*) established a rapport
between the two that gave Mankiewicz an opportunity to understand her temperament and unique personality as have few people
who have known her.

WALTER WANGER: At sixty-nine, trim, dapper, jaunty, the producer
of *Cleopatra* and the very picture of film producer as aristocrat.
Wanger originated the idea of "let's get Liz Taylor to be Cleo" as
a fitting chapter end but not finish to a long, colorful career in the
film business.

CHARLES EINFELD: Vice-president in charge of advertising, publicity and exploitation for 20th Century-Fox throughout the time covered by the *Papers*, and for some years before. At sixty, the prototype of the tough, dynamic advertising-publicity executive. Possessed of a driving, almost demonic, round-the-clock obsession to make sure that every possible column inch in any newspaper (plus anything he can get in other media) be devoted to merchandising his film. For relief, he applies the same passion to tennis. Rarely has the demanding Mr. Einfeld not reproached his staff for permitting a film to open "on rubber heels," i.e., quietly. Most of the film industry's top advertising-publicity executives have been, at one time or another, members of that staff and would no doubt admit—as do the authors—to maintaining a certain amount of reverence for the man who "taught us all we know." More often than not, Mr. Einfeld is referred to as Charlie.

SHEILAH GRAHAM: The noted Hollywood columnist and author, whose book *Beloved Infidel*, recounting her years with F. Scott Fitzgerald, was filmed some years ago by 20th Century-Fox, had no official connection with the production of *Cleopatra*, but her frequent reappearance in these pages dictates her inclusion as a "principal."

W. C. MICHEL: A tight-fisted cigar chomper, who rose from the corporate ranks of 20th Century-Fox to become the company's executive vice-president and, for a time after the Wall Street interests took a degree of control, co-holder with Spyros P. Skouras of the power to make the important decisions of the company.

JOSEPH H. MOSKOWITZ: Vice-president of 20th Century-Fox and Eastern studio representative. Michel and Moskowitz, in whom a great deal of power dwelt, on the whole sided neither with Skouras nor the Wall Street faction trying to gain complete control. The two, colleagues for many years, are referred to occasionally as M&M. They are not to be confused with those other two powerhouses, Mantle and Maris.

SPYROS P. SKOURAS: At the start of our story the president of 20th Century-Fox. In his mid-sixties, one of the world's all too few authentic celebrities and individuals. A fiery Greek *and* American patriot, and always capable of being in at least two places at once. He has been simultaneously cheered as the motion picture industry's savior (via the introduction of the wide-screen process known as CinemaScope at a time when television had all but clubbed the film business to its knees) and blamed for the staggering losses suffered by Fox (100 million dollars is a conservative estimate for the last few years), due to the brink-of-disaster level of *Cleopatra's* costs and a plethora of bad pictures. He is variously referred to as the Old Greek, SPS, Papa (with no lack of the affectionate implication) and some other recognizable familiars.

PETER G. LEVATHES: Fortyish, originally a trainee and disciple of Skouras. He had left Fox to make his mark in the advertising agency business and had then returned to the company to head its television production activities. At the time our story begins, he had become the choice of anti-Skouras elements and had ascended to a vice-presidency as the executive in charge of production (theatrical as well as television films), a title never completely owned by those who had come between Darryl F. Zanuck and himself.

RICHARD BURTON: Richard, Dickie, RB and Burton all signify this actor who enjoyed world-wide repute before he ever stepped into one of Antony's togas. A man whose fame as a personality has now exceeded his renown as an actor, Burton was, the authors feel, the most colorful of the *Cleo* participants. His wife, Sybil, is another character in the drama, a self-explanatory one.

DARRYL F. ZANUCK: Former production chief of 20th Century-Fox, who had left the post some years earlier to head his own independent production company releasing through Fox. Still the largest single stockholder in Fox, during the course of our story he interrupted his devotion to his current production, *The Longest Day*, to re-enter the ranks of the troubled corporation.

REX HARRISON: The third star on the *Cleo* marquee, another actor with a great and deserved reputation, and the leading man Miss Taylor did *not* fall in love with. There is not a great deal about Harrison in the *Papers*, not because his contribution to the film was less than anyone else's, but because he was constantly overshadowed by two more flamboyant personalities. The authors wish to say that they felt all along this would be corrected by the first public showing of the film.

AND

THE BOAT: A designation which appears in these pages for a man whose name cannot be used. This was the code employed throughout the correspondence to represent the gentleman who worked mightily to reveal and correct the difficulties then engulfing 20th Century-Fox.

■■

"This picture was conceived in a state of emergency, shot in confusion, and wound up in blind panic."

—JOSEPH L. MANKIEWICZ

■■

"A man who comes through that ordeal of fire in Rome must emerge a different or a better man."

—RICHARD BURTON

■■

"I don't pretend to be an ordinary housewife. I am not and couldn't be."

—ELIZABETH TAYLOR

■■

"Nothing is as cheap as a hit no matter how much it costs."

—WALTER WANGER

■■

PART ONE

PART ONE

■■■■■■■■■■■■■

Rome, October 1, 1961

Dear Jack,

I have seen *Cleopatra.* I mean I have seen it starting. They began on September 25, but as you know we didn't get here until a couple of days later. Last night was one of the most thrilling of my life. Golda [Weiss's wife] and I went to a location filming of a scene being shot at an encampment at the foot of high cliffs down the road from Rome, on the way to Anzio. Right at the water's edge. Fantastic blending of sets with the natural seacoast. Went down to Anzio yesterday to see the fabulous Alexandrian sets they are building down there, and these on top of the magnificent Roman sets at the studio in Cinecittà are really something. They have character and strength—and they are not just sets, as in dear old Hollywood.

Last night was my first chance to see radiantly beautiful Elizabeth Taylor hard at work. Spent a few minutes on set with Joe Mankiewicz. Walter Wanger took us out there, and he gave me the first 130 pages of Mank's script to read so that I could talk intelligently about it to Joe tonight. It will be the most truly brilliant treatment of history in terms of people and not merely in terms of spectacle that the movies have ever attempted.

Terribly excited about the news of our first major *Life* break on the picture.

I think everything indicates that salvation lies ahead. But there is a problem here, and the only solution that I can see is that you come to Rome and take over the American publicity direction on this film for the duration. What is your reaction? I will hold the fort in New York without you if you are willing to take this on. With the company's very life at stake and riding on this picture, I think it is the right thing to do. For you and Dorothy [Brodsky's wife] it would be an experience—the film, living abroad, all the rest of it—of a lifetime, and one I would envy. But I talked to Charlie in Paris—he would not of course permit me to do it, nor can I do it—but he would be willing to let you be reassigned if agreeable to you. Think it over, as, if we are to do it, I think you should come over soon, before they get deeply into production, and even before I get back to the States. Let me hear from you.

Best regards,
Nat

3

■■■■■■■■■■■■

Dear Nat,

There are so many impressions of the place and of things which have happened that I'll just reel off things as they come to me. The production is really fabulous. The sets are beyond description, particularly the Forum which is bigger than the original and about 100 times as expensive. I have seen some rushes already and it all looks wonderful. Taylor works in the Procession tomorrow, the scene where she is drawn through the Forum arch by 300 slaves. It's one of the big scenes in the picture and when that's done, we can relax a bit. She looks gorgeous, seems to have lost weight and in general is behaving quite nicely.

She refused to see Sheilah Graham when she was here and this may boomerang into a rough piece by Sheilah, but nobody here is giving much thought to that now. Everyone has one purpose—get the picture made, made well and into a theater as soon as possible.

Mank is a true perfectionist and it looks as if we may be here for quite a while. No one can believe we're going to spend ten million on the picture, but the sets alone look that much. Wanger told me the cost may go over ten. Can Fox stand it?

Speaking of our dear old Alma Mater, I do want to apologize for leaving you at the mercy of the gang on the third floor, but someone had to come here. At any rate, I'm sure you can cope. Keep me up to date on the Fox politics. It should be an interesting winter.

If I sound uncertain, I'm really not. We both knew when you wrote that letter that this had to be done. At any rate, the film should be finished in March. It's certainly worth a few months to try to establish *Cleopatra* the way she should be established. And maybe the company will right itself and we will stay with the ship. Pardon the daydreaming, but it would be fun to see Fox get back on its feet, wouldn't it?

Love,
Jack

4

■■■■■■■■■■■■■

New York, October 18

Dear Jack,

It was wonderful to hear from you and to know that you and Dorothy are safe on the ground. You know my fear of flying and how nervous it makes me to even watch someone get on a plane.

I envy you the Roman experience. Now that Taylor is back to health, things should go smoothly.

As for the situation here, it is even more frantic than when you left. Michel and Moskowitz seem to be gaining the power that is fast slipping from Skouras' grasp. It is hard to imagine him shorn of his grandeur. Charlie is having his own problems. As for how long SPS can last, it's anybody's guess. Unless he can have *Cleo* ready in a hurry, he'll be out on his fanny. As it is, The Boat says SPS is through. The Boat said he told Skouras a year ago that if he did not name Levathes his successor soon, they would bury him. SPS agreed, says The Boat, but I can't quite see Levathes in the job. Can you?

The Boat tells me he came up with the idea of not one, but two *Cleopatras*. They'll have Caesar and Cleopatra for next year and Antony and Cleo for the following year. They say here that the pic will cost closer to 20 million when they're through and that this way, Fox can have two blockbusters at ten million each. That's why Levathes is on his way to Rome now, to talk Mank into it. Will write more soon.

Love,
Nat

5

....

OCTOBER 20   WEISS   NEW YORK
YOURE KIDDING STOP TWO CLEOPATRAS QUESTION MARK
SO FAR WE ARE HAVING ENOUGH TROUBLE GETTING ONE
STOP WRITING DETAILS FRETFULLY BRODSKY

Dear Nat,

Now I know you're not kidding. Burton told me Skouras and Levathes asked him whether he'd mind terribly if they finished the picture when Caesar is killed. "I told them I'd sue them until they're puce," he told me.

The weather has turned dreadful. We're supposed to finish the outdoor shooting by November, but with this weather, it's almost impossible. We can't get that one day's shooting on the Sphinx and that is holding up some of my publicity material. You can't very well have stories on the Procession without Taylor and you can't have Taylor until the weather clears. You don't want to highlight the intimate stuff yet, because this will look as if we don't have the spectacle. So there we are. I'm fighting a delaying action with the *Times, Newsweek, Time,* etc., in order to get the Taylor Procession shot out of the way. But the preliminary stuff is breaking pretty well and I feel the world is beginning to learn about *Cleo.* I've been getting some snide digs from New York about the need to step up the publicity. I realize they're all desperate, but don't they realize I've only been here a relatively few days?

Anyway, as you must know, Dorothy is desperate for Sam [the Brodskys' four-year-old cocker spaniel]. Would you please see what you can do about getting him on a plane as quickly as possible? He is a most important member of the family.

As for work, there is still chaos, organized chaos, but chaos nevertheless. The inter-office and inter-crew politics are intriguing but best stayed away from. There are teams here, the way there are teams everywhere, but the only team to be on is the Mankiewicz team. Right now I'm a substitute outfielder on that team; the manager doesn't know what I can do. I'm hoping to make the first team in time and I'll keep you up to date.

Personally, we've adjusted pretty well. We've taken a small apartment in one of the well-known residence hotels in Parioli, about 15 minutes from the Via Veneto and 45 from Cinecittà. We have a half-ass duplex, with a living room (if you can call it that) downstairs and bedroom and bathroom upstairs. Unfortunately, we live next door to a young lady who arrives home about 3 every morning with a friend in tow. The walls are pizza-thin and we can

7

hear every sound. Educational, if not sleep inducing. The neighborhood is kind of pleasant, with a shopkeeper up the street whom
Dorothy has already dubbed Jessica James, if that gives you an idea
about Italian shopkeepers.

   We'll adjust, I think.

Love,

Jack

OCTOBER 26 WEISS NEW YORK
HOW ARE YOU PROGRESSING SAM STOP REMEMBER HE
NERVOUS ANIMAL STOP WOULD HATE TO SEE ANY MISHAP
IN AIR STOP AM HOLDING YOU RESPONSIBLE HIS SAFETY
WORRIEDLY JACK

OCTOBER 27 BRODSKY ROME
SAM WILL ARRIVE ROME TWA FLIGHT 901 SATURDAY MORN-
ING STOP AS NEAR AS I CAN TELL HE IN GOOD PHYSICAL
CONDITION ANXIOUSLY AWAITING TRIP STOP AS FOR NERVES
CANNOT HOLD HIS PAW IN FLIGHT BUT WILL GIVE HIM
SAME TRANQUILIZER I TAKE STOP LET ME KNOW HOW HE
TAKES IT LOVE NAT

OCTOBER 29 WEISS NEW YORK
THANK GOD SAM ARRIVED IN GREAT SHAPE STOP PLEASE
NOTIFY MY MOTHER STOP TAKING DOG TORRE ASTURA THIS
WEEKEND SEE CLEO ALEXANDRIAN PALACE SET STOP TRIED
GET HIM SPOT IN PROCESSION BUT MANKIEWICZ IS WITHOUT
REAL SENSE OF HUMOR LOVE JACK

Rome, November 5

Dear Nat,

Thank you for your help with Sam. He arrived in fine shape, as I cabled you, none the worse for wear and with his little flight bag tied to his kennel. When the TWA people removed him from his kennel he and Dorothy had a scene, something like the kind of thing Ralph Edwards used to have on "This Is Your Life." You remember, when the mother hadn't seen her child who'd been in a concentration camp? That's my wife. She slobbered over him for a few minutes, mumbling "My baby, my baby," and the attendants seemed touched. I wanted to hide. When one of them asked Dorothy how long it had been since she'd seen her dog, she started to say "Two weeks," and at the height of her sobs, I stopped her at the "two" and said ". . . years."

Love,
Jack

■■■■■■■■■■■■

Dear Nat,

Haven't heard from anyone on a personal level in days. Still getting the blasts about no publicity and am stepping up the guns. Please continue to dynamite the stuff as you have been doing with the boys.

According to the Mank, Skouras said to him, "You've got to give me a budget under ten million." Joe said, "You're crazy, let's be realists, this will cost closer to fifteen." Now Skouras is complaining to Joe that he's going over budget when Joe has never said that the budget would be under ten.

Anyway, as the material breaks around the country, would you please, personally, make it your business to show Mr. Skouras each and every break? We are in the same situation now that we were in with *Francis of Assisi* in those awful first few weeks. No one believes that anything is going to appear in print and there's a tremendous amount of consternation on Michel, Moskowitz and Skouras' part. Please keep shoving the material under their noses. I am out to make *Francis of Assisi* and *The Longest Day* look like *Madison Avenue* [a small-budget, unheralded picture that contributed to former production chief Bob Goldstein's downfall] as far as publicity is concerned. Mark my words, this will be the most publicized picture of all time.

Love,
Jack

■■■■■■■■■■■■

New York, November 15, 1961

Dear Jack,

I'm trying, I'm trying. Listen, they're all running in six directions at once. If you were losing 20 to 25 million this year, you'd be nervous, too. Right now, we're all concerned with Selznick and Jennifer Jones arriving for *Tender Is the Night*. Levathes is making statements that this is our Academy Award pic. Levathes for president. I showed off—in answer to the complaints on no *Cleo* publicity—this week's *Life*, *Newsweek*, Sunday *Times* Magazine, Kilgallen, Skolsky, Wilson, but it didn't seem to dent anyone.

The battle lines seem to be drawing here. I think Robert Lehman will be the deciding factor on the board. The Skouras job, if indeed he is to resign, is still up for grabs.

Relax, it doesn't pay to get that involved with *Cleo*, it's Taylor who has the ten per cent.

Love,

Nat

P.S. Saw *The Comancheros* last night. We may not make it 'til Christmas.

N.

Dear Nat,

I'm not the only one with pressure. And who can keep from being involved? Not only is New York still complaining about no publicity, but they keep crabbing about Sheilah Graham and are intent upon screwing Mankiewicz up. Mankiewicz has a chance at making a great film and at this rate they may very well foul him up. You must see the logic about letting him make the picture his way. Sure, there may be people who are careless with dough and have to be sat on—as Sid Rogell [Fox executive] has done an excellent job of—but to get Mank to cut out scenes or to try to impose a heavier work schedule, as Levathes and Skouras are doing, is preposterous. If they persist, they will get an inferior product. Wanger said as much in a recent meeting with Skouras and got his ass blasted off. Skouras was very warm with me, then cracked that there's no publicity. Oh, well.

The crew hates the six-day work week we're on and they don't function as well as they should. If Skouras would relent, I'm sure Mank would get more done in five days. Taylor is violent in her feelings on five versus six days and told Joe M. today: "Let's just not show up. What can they do, fire us?" She does not really understand her own power in this picture and never really acts like ELIZABETH TAYLOR. She and Fisher seem very much in love, if you can ever find them amid the sycophants and hangers-on who have latched onto them.

We have really settled down and, believe it or not, we're enjoying it immensely. Except for the slight Einfeld harassment, we are reacting as you might imagine we would to everything. And the combination of the film and living in Rome is an exotic one. True, I am beat every night and the sixth day troubles me as much as it does Joe and Elizabeth (a name dropper?), but there is something about the whole goddamned project which is fascinating. Dottie has also adapted and but for her worry, occasionally, that her mother is terribly lonesome, she is having a ball. Remember, Dorothy is an absolute nut for Italian food and has finally begun to gain weight. I have lost some, if you can imagine that. Even Skouras commented on it.

We take tremendous delight in going out to the restaurants, and our evenings are usually full of warmth, good food and pleasant feeling. Yesterday we just spent the afternoon wandering around the Colosseum and Forum, had lunch overlooking the Forum, came home, napped, and went out for dinner with Bob Penn [the still photographer] and his wife Sheila at a wonderful new tavern we discovered. All in all a marvelous Sunday.

Love,
Jack

■ ■ ■ ■ ■ ■ ■ ■ ■ ■ ■ ■

Rome, November 23

Dear Nat,

We're moving! Still no Procession, but Mank has his five-day week and everyone seems much happier. Now, enough of this business. I have an important request. Richard Burton is coming to New York over the weekend to tape a TV spec. I've prevailed upon him to carry back some corned beef and salami from the Stage Delicatessen. Please call [restaurateur] Max Asnas and see that Burton gets it to bring back. I've alerted him that he'd hear from you. Mankiewicz will share in the goodies, so, for the good of the film, come through.

Love,
Jack

NOVEMBER 27   WEISS   NEW YORK
WHERE IS MY CORNED BEEF STOP BURTON SAYS YOU NEVER
CONTACTED HIM STOP OUR FRIENDSHIP IS AT AN END
UNLESS EXPLANATION REASONABLE STOP WEATHER HAS
STALLED PROCESSION INDEFINITELY AT COST OF SEVERAL
HUNDRED THOUSAND BUT THIS DROP IN BUCKET COMPARED
ANGUISH YOU CAUSED ME AND FOUR TIME ACADEMY AWARD
WINNER STOP COOLLY BRODSKY

NOVEMBER 28   BRODSKY   ROME
PRESS OF DUTIES PLUS POLITICAL INFIGHTING PLUS NEAR
FATAL HEAD COLD CAUSED DELI MIXUP STOP HAVE SHIPPED
WITH ASSISTANT CAMERAMAN ARRIVING TODAY WILL CON-
TACT YOU YOUR FRIEND NAT

NOVEMBER 29   WEISS   NEW YORK
YOUR CLEO CONTRIBUTION ARRIVED AND AIDED AWARD
WINNING WRITER DIRECTOR IN WRITING MAGNIFICENT
ANTONY CLEO SCENE STOP IF LOVE SCENE AS GOOD AS
CORNED BEEF PICTURE MUST TOP GONE WITH WIND
STOP I FORGIVE YOU LOVE JACK

■■■■■■■■■■■■

Dear Jack,

Bulletin: Today's board meeting is over and financial statement shows more whopping losses. The scuttlebutt is that Skouras may resign January 1—where have I heard that before?—but may prefer to do it around May 1, by which time, he says, company will be in better shape, and it won't look as if he's been fired. Board seemed to feel if he resists they'll wait for peaceful May 1 settlement rather than get out the tar and feathers. I'm sure SPS feels he can be saved by having *Cleo* in time to open just after the 1962 stockholders' meeting.

Love,
Nat

■■■■■■■■■■■■

Dear Jack,

Spent much of the weekend on the phone with The Boat. He feels there's no chance that Jerry Wald will get the production job, which I had suggested to him time and again. *Adventures of a Young Man* is going way over budget. The Boat thinks Charlie's thought that Zanuck might get into the act soon is not too far-fetched.

The Boat tells me that at the last board meeting [Wall Street board member and lawyer Milton] Gould and Michel had it out. The feeling is that there will be a fight to keep Michel from gaining power. But Levathes' position is such that he can't muster enough support. So who?

Skouras is trying to get a reel of film on *Cleo* to show to exhibitors around the country as soon as possible. The gimmick will be to get stockholders to attend these showings to rally them behind him to try to rescue his presidency come May 1st. See what you can do to nudge Liz, huh?

Love,
Nat

■ ■ ■ ■ ■ ■ ■ ■ ■ ■ ■ ■

DECEMBER 10   WEISS   NEW YORK
DO SKOURAS EINFELD SEE ALL CLIPPINGS CHARLIES LETTERS
DONT REFLECT THIS BRODSKY

■■■■■■■■■■■■

Dear Nat,

Since you are fighting so many battles, perhaps you can help fight one of mine. I realize there must be pressure on Charlie but his letters get more frantic by the day and although I suspect your handiwork in getting some moderation into them, it is more than I can bear.

First of all, he ought to stop on the Graham business. How can he blame us when Taylor refused to see her? Doesn't he understand that you are dealing with Elizabeth Taylor, Rex Harrison and Joe Mankiewicz, not Stephen Boyd and Dolores Hart? Mankiewicz is not giving interviews only because he hasn't got a single minute to give interviews. As for Taylor and Harrison, they do what they think is important. The *Newsweek* break was gained with Harrison's cooperation, the *Times* layout with hers. As for *Show Business Illustrated*, I could not even show that to the Fishers. They have absolutely no sense of humor about their personal lives.

And those Zanuck-Einfeld letters! Zanuck writes Charlie that *Day* publicity is 3-1 ahead of *Cleo* in England and Europe, and Charlie simply accepts it. Didn't somebody stop to check? I think the inmates have taken over the asylum in New York. How the hell does Zanuck know what *Cleo* is doing in England? Or Italy? Or Germany? We've been pouring out the feature stories, dealing with the correspondents, building the picture tremendously. And the clippings we are seeing are staggering. Presumably Zanuck only sees his own clippings from countries outside France!

To give you an idea of the absurdity of these complaints, Wanger saw both their letters—he sees everything, is always around reading—and really laughed. He told Mank and Joe broke up too. Mank is firmly convinced that the letter from Charlie was written so that Charlie could send a copy to Zanuck to show him that he's not neglecting *Day*. I, for one, am convinced that Zanuck's complex about *Day* and *Cleo* publicity is enormous. But there's not much he can do about it.

Right now I'll stake all the corned beef in the world that we're murdering *Day*. I'll say it again, by the time *Cleo* is finished, it will have set a mark for publicity that nothing will ever follow—co-operation or no.

Love,

Jack

P.S. Forgot to tell you great story: Friday, Harrison told his dresser, "Put this in my trailer." He has trailer, as does Taylor, outside sound stage and this acts as sort of portable dressing room. Dresser says, "You don't have a trailer any more. Rogell took it away. Economy." (He's the economy man here, you know, firing people right and left and cutting costs to the bone.) Harrison went up in flames, stopped being made up and told everyone he was going back to England. Wanger and Mankiewicz came to watch the storm and Harrison yelled, "Send Rogell here immediately." Rogell was sent for and Harrison said to him, "I treat my servants better than I am about to treat you." Then he launched into a tirade of some choice Anglo-Saxon expletives (a few I'd never heard and remember I took my basic training in Arkansas) and told him that if he didn't have the %$#"&')$) trailer back in 15 minutes, he (Rex) was on his way back to England. Rogell said OK and Harrison kicked him out. When Harrison went out on the set, he was applauded by the entire cast and crew.

Love again,

JB

....

New York, December 12

Dear Jack,

Spent a zany, Marx Brothers day with Einfeld and Skouras. The big problem of the day, it seems, is that Mrs. Skouras wants to send a Christmas card after all, after the annual Xmas card had been by-passed this year—the Skourases are turning down Christmas as a material if not spiritual economy. Only now Mr. S. wants to send out a Company Xmas card, whatever that is, from him and Mrs. S. (the company will foot the bill)—a message, for instance, about clean, wholesome entertainment for the whole family from 20th Century-Fox, and season's greetings from Mr. and Mrs. Spyros P. Skouras. Makes sense.

We haven't seen *Tender Is the Night* as yet, although the Selznicks have been here for weeks. Will see pic tomorrow, but saw the trailer today and it's not to be believed—this middle-aged, twitching woman (a serious Alice Pearce) rolling on floors, on beds, on beaches in clinch after clinch with world-weary, gray, lined and creased Jason Robards, Jr. (JUNIOR!) It's going to hurt this company, I tell you! How goes the epic? Your stuff seems to be breaking well.

Love,
Nat

■■■■■■■■■■■■

Dear Nat,

Today was the kind of day that makes some of these trials and tribulations seem worth it. We shot a nude scene of Miss Taylor being rubbed by one of her handmaidens on a marble slab in her apartment. The set was ordered closed, with only a minimum number of technicians allowed. I just happened to stroll on and stood next to Bob Penn, who was told that his negatives were to be given directly to Wanger. I waited for someone to chase me, and I already had my story prepared about how important it was to my work, but Mank probably figured, "Give the kid a break." Anyway, Liz was adjusted by Eddie himself and the crew seemed to be occupied with what they were doing. Bob Penn snapped away and I sort of shuffled from one foot to another, trying to look business-like. My Adam's apple seemed to be straining at my throat.

The next day, we delivered the negatives and prints to Eddie and Liz and I looked over their shoulders as they scanned the material. It's quite an experience, looking at naked photos of a guy's wife, with the wife and husband present. Liz won't allow them in print, save, she says, for one page in *Vogue* or *Harper's Bazaar*. Eddie nodded and so did I. Maybe the fashion will catch on.

Love,
Jack

■■■■■■■■■■■■

DECEMBER 15   BRODSKY   ROME
BOAT STEAMING INTO PORT HOPEFULLY WEISS

DECEMBER 15   WEISS   NEW YORK
WHAT THE HELL DOES THAT MEAN BRODSKY

24

Dear Jack,

Thought I was being perfectly clear. The Boat tells me SPS is definitely out, only a matter of time, and that he and his Wall Street cronies are going to get everything they wanted. Boat into port, see?

Saw *Tender* finally, then one of those wild ad-pub boardroom sessions where everyone lied about how great it is. SPS read us wires from Selznick telling us we're idiots not to show it for the Academy Awards. It is so awful. Can Henry King [the film's director] have read the book? Don't they know this isn't Fannie Hurst, man, this is Scott Fitzgerald?

I think I may have calmed Skouras down. I waylaid him with enough publicity breaks to give anyone a hernia. It may be that he's desperate for a friend or something, but it finally dawned on him that the world is beginning to know about *Cleo*. He even talked about writing you a nice letter. Imagine?

Have just been through the worst four-day period in recent memory. The worst. All that I could do was a) maneuver Skouras, b) influence Einfeld, c) get all the "official" work done in those areas, d) open two pictures in the next four days, e) spend all available time with Jack Clayton [producer-director of Fox's *The Innocents*], f) work out the biggest opening New York ever saw for *Tender*, g) work out our personnel problems, h) work out a fantastic and devious procedure to permit us to give Xmas presents to our most important contacts, which had been forbidden, and i) dogged Skouras' heels about a reception he cooked up for Clayton on 24 hours' notice. I managed this all and delivered 175 people, including about 40 top names like Jerome Robbins, Joan Fontaine, Nathan Milstein, Maurice Evans, plus most of the top critics. All was fine except the host [Skouras] didn't show and Einfeld walked out because Clayton didn't agree with his advertising concept. To top it all off, Michel is planning an SPS 25th anniversary sales drive—suddenly it's 1910.

But don't get me wrong, I love 20th Century-Fox.

Love,

Nat

P.S. As I wrote you from the office, hope you have good luck in getting Taylor to pose with the issue of *McCall's* that has her on the cover. We could certainly use all the space that *McCall's* has promised, to counteract the "not enough publicity" line.

NW

···········

DECEMBER 22   BRODSKY   ROME
SAW YOUR CABLE TO EINFELD ABOUT MCCALLS PIX TURN-
ING OUT BADLY STOP SMELLS FISHY STOP WRITE ME REAL
STORY STOP WEISS

DECEMBER 22   WEISS   NEW YORK
YOURE DAMN RIGHT ITS FISHY STOP WRITING TRUTH FOR
YOUR EYES ONLY BRODSKY

Dear Nat,

I'll try to give you a blow-by-blow description of *l'affaire Mc-Call's*, but keep it confidential. I never worked as hard to get anything in my life and the vision of those goddamned full pages in the papers had my mouth watering. It began with my getting the letter from the *McCall's* editor and the magazine on Tuesday, and my meeting first with Dick Hanley, her secretary, and Fisher, and then with *her*. She first didn't think she ought to do it, then said she'd read the article and let me know. Then Eddie calls me to say OK. So I have to submit ideas for how she'll do it. I submit the ideas and she doesn't like any of them. (All this is spread over a few days, mind you.) I keep telling them the deadline for taking the pic is Friday. By Thursday, after I have hounded her from one end of Cinecittà to the other, she says she won't do it as Cleo, only as herself. Mank gets in the act, finally, and says, "I think she ought to do it, but not as Cleo." That cinched that. However, I figured taking it on the set with a camera nearby would cinch a plug in the copy. Then she says she doesn't like the way her hair looks. And she doesn't have time to wash it. Maybe Friday evening after shooting? I spend all day Friday chasing her and at 5:30 Friday we are on the set and she is in a gorgeous outfit—pink slacks, a terrific shirt and a kerchief, looking like a zillion dollars. She says, "I may wash my hair in half an hour, then we'll take the pix in my dressing room." I press for them now and Mankiewicz comes to my aid. Says he, "Sit down and take it." (To digress for a moment, he is her Svengali.) So she sits down and Leon Shamroy [cinematographer on the film]—I love him—lights it. Can you imagine, seven or eight Academy Awards working on the shot and Mankiewicz directs it! I was flipping. We took great shots and left happy. I took the stuff into the lab with Bob Penn, made arrangements with a TWA pilot to bring it Sunday. The next day (Saturday, yesterday) I had to bring them to the villa to show her, since she has absolute approval on everything. Fisher comes down in a bathrobe (it's about 11:00 A.M.) and tells me he'll bring them up to her, she's still in bed. (Tired from counting her money.) He comes back in half an hour, saying she's changed her mind, she doesn't want to do it now. I controlled myself and argued quietly, but to no avail.

He says he argued with her, but the answer is no. I went back to Rome, called Mank who said he wouldn't intervene any more, talked to Wanger who did make a token call to Fisher, but all was lost. Then Wanger told me to blame the pictures. That's the story. A great business? And you know something? I don't care about *Tender Is the Night*.

Love,
Jack

P.S. Merry Christmas.

P.P.S. The first 50 pages of the second act have just come from Mank's pen and they're fabulous. Burton and Taylor will set off sparks, and already Fisher is jealous of the lines Burton has. Richard has a magnificent speech, wherein he tells Cleopatra of his torment at having to follow in Caesar's image all his life, at being beset by ghosts and shadows of Caesar wherever he goes. Great stuff. What a picture. (Watch it die.)

JB

New York, December 26

Dear Jack,

Wanger, here for Xmas, told me things you had been keeping from me: That *Cleo* has a lot longer to go than anyone will admit and that Taylor's recurrent leg trouble has forced them to carry her on the set every day for the past several days.

Wanger told me that the extravagance of building the sets (Wanger blames SPS and Skouras blames Wanger) meant a loss of 5 million on the Rome, never mind the London production. He told *Variety* that *Cleo* would cost 18-19 million. Yipe. I can see the stockholders marching on SPS when the paper comes out on Wednesday.

Just before the holiday weekend, Charlie got a desperate idea. We never did open *Tender* for the Academy, and on Friday morning before the Christmas party, Charlie discovers that *The Children's Hour* has opened to poor reviews and business in L.A. and that's the theater where *Tender* is to open in February. An idea forms in his mind, and for the next few hours we are driven mad trying to do the following: Charlie says "now that *Children's Hour* is a flop we can get them to step aside, bounce the pic after a four-day run, and open *Tender* in that house to let *it* take its turn at qualifying for the Academy Awards." Please note that by the rules it must open 7 days before December 31, that comes to December 24, and at that moment it's noon on the 22nd! And the eve of a long holiday weekend, during which the opening, let alone the advertising of it, must take place. By the end of the day Charlie knew he didn't have a prayer.

Hope you had a happy holiday.

Love,
Nat

■ ■ ■ ■ ■ ■ ■ ■ ■ ■ ■ ■

Dear Nat,

Wanger is back and confiding that the picture may really cost close to 25 million by the time it is in the can. Isn't that staggering? He also told me a marvelous story about the deal—with Taylor—falling through at one point, and Fox ready to sign Susan Hayward, make the announcement, everything, until he (Wanger) patched it up.

For Christmas Mankiewicz and Taylor threw a party at a local restaurant. Her leg continues to bother her, so she didn't show. But the party was a good brawl.

Yes, the picture is going slowly. Wanger hints that we may be here until June and that's a little long. I can't believe it will take that long.

Love,
Jack

■■■■■■■■■■■■

New York, December 31

Dear Jack,

Please try to fix it so that Bert Stern can come again or some of the other big magazine photographers. Six months from now we'll want more big magazine breaks and getting these names will help.

We saw something called *Second Time Around* today. Debbie Reynolds. No comment.

Charlie has been behaving like Charlie even more. Being in the Michel-Moskowitz-Skouras vise is no help. He's looking for a new secretary, one without temperament. He wants "somebody who can take a beating." Also "she should look like Madison Avenue and be beautiful." One of the girls countered with: "Maybe *she*, whoever she is, would like to work for Cary Grant."

Love,
Nat

■ ■ ■ ■ ■ ■ ■ ■ ■ ■ ■ ■

[*The next several weeks proved uneventful, with the Fox situation in New York at a standstill. Judge Samuel Rosenman, a famed jurist, noted as a speech writer for FDR, was elected chairman of the board of 20th Century-Fox in an apparent move to mollify all the dissidents. It had been rumored in the trade press that Michel might supplant Skouras as a temporary president before the appointment of Levathes, with Skouras moving up to board chairman. Now the presence of Rosenman in the latter post closed off that possibility. The press then speculated that Skouras would remain nominally president; Rosenman would "preside" at board meetings, and Michel would "chair" them. Skouras tried hard to prod the Cleopatra makers into rushing ahead on film, but Mankiewicz, intent on his craft, would not be hurried. Rex Harrison's role in the film was near completion and Richard Burton began filming his scenes with Elizabeth Taylor. It was the first time that Taylor and Burton were to work in close proximity. The first few days were punctuated with quotes from Burton on his co-star's eyes. Then rumors of hurried visits by Wanger and Mankiewicz to the Fisher household were heard, and the storm of rumors surrounding Taylor and Burton grew wilder. The film continued to progress slowly and in February was just about half completed. On February 14, Brodsky's wife, Dorothy, was given the news that she was to become a mother in September. That evening, Brodsky telephoned Weiss in New York.*]

BRODSKY: Nathan, I've got a surprise for you.

WEISS: Dorothy's pregnant.

BRODSKY: How the hell did you know? I just found out.

WEISS: Intuition, it's the fountains or something. Anyway, congratulations.

BRODSKY: We're overjoyed, but Dorothy isn't too well. The food is taking its toll and the doctor is giving her all kinds of injections.

WEISS: Jack, there are rumors around New York about Burton, Taylor and Fisher. Why haven't you written?

BRODSKY: I took an oath in blood. They think it may be the end of the picture.

WEISS: My God, you mean it's true?

BRODSKY: I'll write tomorrow, but keep it to yourself. Everyone's trying to stop it.

WEISS: Well, congratulations again.

BRODSKY: You can see, can't you, the fountains weren't the inspiration.

Rome, February 15

Dear Nat,

It's no rumor, no guesswork, about what Burton is doing to Taylor. It's plain fact. It started about three weeks ago and is now the hottest thing ever. It seems that Fisher found out about it and started squawking, so Taylor said, quote, I love him and I want to marry him, unquote. Mank, Wanger, not to mention Fisher, died. Burton has told Taylor he wants her, too, but Wanger believes Burton will never leave his wife. Fisher, it seems, still loves her, is hung on her and the kids. He has taken off for Switzerland. Isn't that incredible?

Nobody wants this to get out because they feel that the public will crucify her and picket the theaters if she breaks up another family. Burton, on the other hand, is having a ball, and told a friend with whom he's worked on other pix, "She'll be on the set every fucking day I'm on." True to tell, yesterday Taylor wasn't working, Fisher went to Switzerland, and she came down to watch Burton work and was the life of the party, bubbling all around. They sneak off at night to an apartment and have matinees in her dressing room. It is the talk of the studio and Rome. It's too much. What we clearly must do is to bottle it up as long as we can. I'll keep you informed of the details, but at this point things could go any which way. One day Taylor is bubbling, the next remorseful. Forget anything you guys want her to do for a long time.

I had a cable from Skouras congratulating us on the impending blessed event and suggesting we name the baby Julius, Cleo, or, he said, Spyros. Spyros Brodsky. Personally, *I* like it.

Love,

Jack

■■■■■■■■■■■■

FEBRUARY 17   BRODSKY   ROME
PERRY COMO SHOW HAD TAKEOFF ON CLEO WITH SLAVE
NAMED EDDIE GETTING IN ANTONYS WAY STOP DO THEY
KNOW BEST WEISS

36

Dear Nat,

I just saw the ad in the Sunday *Times* on *Satan Never Sleeps*, and it needs no comment. It is the incredible ad of all time. A Chinese girl raped in front of a priest and Fox is trying to tell the world it's another *Going My Way!!*

Now to business, or rather, to monkey business. On Wednesday, Taylor comes on the set when Burton is working. She's gay, vivacious, smiling. I'm ready to ask her about Bert Stern. I tell her Dottie is expecting, she's thrilled. (Burton offered to be the godfather, tell Golda that and watch her eyes flash steel.) I digress. So she's thrilled. Everything's ducky. Then Roddy McDowall [playing the role of Octavian in the film] comes on the set. He's been in between everyone, you might know, because of his various friendships. He tells Burton that Sybil is about to blow the joint. Burton pales. He loves his wife after a fashion, and hanky-panky or no, she and the kids come first. However, she blows town (ostensibly to see his sick father in New York) but the word is that she is not giving this the go-by. Taylor dies, she turned white on the set when Burton took her into his dressing room to tell her the news.

Anyway she goes wild on Friday when Burton tells her it was great fun, but it was just one of those things. Mank and WW try to calm her down but she's coconuts. She wants to junk everything. Imagine, a guy turning her down! Already Fisher has moved out, is in Lisbon at that moment doing a TV show (he's thinner than anybody has a right to be and is existing on fruit juices). Comes Saturday night and Miss Taylor lands in the hospital. At 3:00 A.M., Reynolds Packard, the Rome correspondent of the *Daily News*, wakes me up to ask me what's cooking. The whole world is in front of the hospital and they want to know. I never got back to sleep. I spent the rest of the night on the phone with WW, AP, UPI, Packard and the whole world, it seemed. WW explained to me what had happened at the house and we agreed to say nothing that night, to talk with her doctor in the morning, around eight.

First thing in the morning, I get a call. A voice says, "This is the B'nai B'rith *News*. What's the story?" It's WW and he's making jokes yet. My pregnant wife is supposed to be getting her rest and the phone is ringing all night. What a life. Anyway, we devised the food poisoning story and it seemed to go over. I tried to call you all day Sunday but no answer.

So today she comes out of the hospital, all smiles. At the same time, Burton's press agents release a story, or rather a statement, saying that Burton denies these rumors about himself and Taylor. (We had successfully stopped people from printing the rumors—a great PR job, I might add—through various ruses and ploys.) So, of course, the papers and wire services jumped on the statement, linked it to the hospital, and at this moment are filing stories on it which you will have seen. When we called Charlie to tell him, he seemed worried that Fox stock might go down.

At this point, nobody knows what will happen with ET and RB. Will she be so angry she'll never speak to him again? Will the affair flare up again in a few days when they begin working again?

Charlie asked me on the phone: "Was it just a bellyache?" I said, "Charlie, we're on the phone." He said, "Write me an air-mail." I can't go through it all again. [Production manager Doc] Merman has told Levathes and Skouras, so you tell Charlie. Only tell him I wrote you all this the day before I spoke to him and then wrote today to tell you to tell him. Clear?

Now to something important: The doctor thinks I ought to get Dottie out of here no later than May 1. Can you think of a solution? I don't want to leave everything hanging here, but my family comes before *Cleo*. Think of something brilliant.

Love,

Jack

■■■■■■■■■■■■

New York, February 22

Dear Jack,

First question: Do we have a picture yet? Are the key scenes shot? From what you say, it looks as if we'll never finish this picture. *The New York Times* said the other day that if Taylor doesn't make it, Fox is lost.

Satan Never Sleeps opened today to record low business. The reviews are enough to begin bankruptcy proceedings here. Desperately, Charlie is trying to get the title song of *Satan Never Sleeps* sung from church pulpits next Sunday. We have time. Today is only Thursday. As for replacing you, I had a brainstorm. Let's switch places. I'm dying to get out of this spot for a few months, Golda would love it, and you'll be able to run things here without me, I'm certain. What think you?

Love,
Nat

■■■■■■■■■■■■

FEBRUARY 24   WEISS   NEW YORK
YOURE CRAZY STOP YOUD HATE IT STOP BUT IF YOU WANT
IT WILL SUGGEST TO CHARLIE STOP LET HIM THINK IT IS
MY IDEA SKEPTICALLY JACK

FEBRUARY 25   BRODSKY   ROME
I WANT IT STOP PAPERS GOING CRAZY LIZ RICHARD STOP
WHATS THE LATEST WEISS

Dear Nat,

Have written to Charlie explaining the need to leave at the end of April and you'll probably see that letter soon. I told him that our switching was the best solution to protect the situation here. But we'll see.

Right now the personal situation is worse than it ever was. Taylor is nuts about Burton and he's on the spot, trying to pacify everyone, but basically wanting to stay married to Sybil. I believe Wanger feels Taylor will wear him down shortly. She has been out ill practically since the day she came back from the hospital. Everyone is trying to act as if nothing had happened but I understand Sybil is ready to leave again, this time with the kids. Certain things, however, are clear.

(1) The Taylor-Fisher marriage is over. It is a matter of days before the lid blows off that. She doesn't want him. (2) They don't have a picture yet. Certain key scenes have yet to be shot. They have a lot shot in Part II already, but some key ones in the Caesar half are missing and who knows when they'll get them the way she's acting. (3) Liz is in a frantic emotional state. Forget, repeat, forget about anything else right now. Let us wait. The situation is crazy.

Burton has offered to be the baby's godfather again, and if it's a boy, we may call him Richard. Do you know that the Oliviers named their baby Richard after him, and he's their son's godfather? The Brodskys and the Oliviers. Can you see us going to their house one night and them coming to ours the next? I'll let you know what we decide.

Love,
Jack

■■■■■■■■■■■■

New York, March 1

Dear Jack,

Today is the day of the big N.Y. to L.A. plane crash and the real problem, according to some people here, is that the print of *State Fair*, due in, will be delayed.

Maybe Taylor and Burton will go on to be the Lunt-Fontanne of their time. Their story has so many possible endings, it will be fascinating to watch. I only hope and pray that it doesn't end before the picture is finished.

The Skouras sales drive is a fiasco. Last night's board meeting was apparently a rough one with a big knockdown dragout between Gould and SPS. SPS has been trying to get cozy with Kennedy, but my sources in Washington tell me that the years of Skouras' supporting Eisenhower and other top Republicans weigh too heavily, and that JFK won't bend. As for the SPS drive, they're way short of the break-even figure. We only have one TV show on next season, a partial by-product of Levathes' move to overall production. We saw *State Fair*, had the usual boardroom session, and I don't have to tell you what a classic it is—no taste, no style, in the great tradition. We're opening with a Medico-Care charity do on a Tuesday, open to the public on Wednesday, with reviews on Thursday. [The company often would open a film in New York on Friday, so that the reviews would appear in the newspapers' Saturday editions which have a notoriously low readership.] Charlie is playing it cagey about my replacing you, but with the film looking like it will go to July, it may work out.

Love,

Nat

P.S. Skouras is talking about booking *Cleopatra* into Madison Square Garden.

■■■■■■■■■■■■

Dear Nat,

As for what really interests you most, we are walking on eggs again with the Burton-Taylor thing, but for some new wrinkles. Honestly, it is so difficult to keep up with this mess, I don't know what to do.

Briefly: Taylor is still mad for him. Meanwhile, Burton is entertaining some Copa cutie over here, an ex-girl friend. Sybil has gone back to New York, no one knows for how long. Taylor and Burton are a riot on the set; she's looking daggers at him, mixed with steamy, passionate stares. He tries to act oblivious to the whole thing. But they had a little tiff almost in the open when she finally couldn't stand it about the Copa cutie. He flaunts her on set all day and Taylor finally made a remark, whereupon Burton pushed her a mite, saying, "Don't get my Welsh temper up." So you can see we're sitting on a powder keg.

Burton came on the set 3 hours late the other day after being out all night. It was a Welsh holiday of some sort. He didn't go home, came into the studio at 7:00 A.M. with the Copa cutie and kept everyone waiting. Taylor said to him—I was there with them at the time and trying to look in any direction but at the two of them—"You kept us all waiting." He says to her, "It's about time somebody kept you waiting. It's a real switch." So Harrison, who is there, too, coughs and says, "Let's rehearse, everyone." Too much.

I asked Mank how he keeps his composure with all that's going on and he says, "When you're in a cage with tigers you never let them know you're afraid of them or they'll eat you."

Love,
Jack

■■■■■■■■■■■■■

Dear Jack,

It never stops. Yesterday we saw *Caligari*, not *the Caligari* but the Bob Lippert reproduction.

[*Lippert made a series of low-budget films for Fox and began to aspire to bigger productions. His remake of the classic horror film was the first pretentious step in that direction. The film was eventually mauled by critics everywhere.*]

Can you imagine a whole series of popular remakes of classics by Bob Lippert? Charlie, deadpan, told the meeting that the picture was better than *Psycho*—which Martin Moskowitz [assistant sales manager and brother of Joseph Moskowitz] thought it only as good as—and Charlie said the picture is baffling and therefore will be all the rage, just like *La Dolce Vita* and *L'Avventura*. SPS said, "You're right, Charlie. We're better than all those Europeans and I don't know why people talk so much about them."

Sudden thought: Do you realize that we have the basis of a Broadway smash in a lightly concealed three-act comedy about the making of *Cleopatra*? Your Sunday piece (for the *Trib*) could be any topic you like; mine (for the *Times*) would talk about the gall of people who try to inherit the mantle of Kaufman and Hart. I'll see what I can do about a theater.

Love,
Nat

P.S. For some reason they've stopped complaining about the lack of publicity.

NW

■■■■■■■■■■■■

[*The next week was one of the most hectic in the off-again, on-again Burton-Taylor-Fisher comedy. Mr. and Mrs. Francis Taylor, Elizabeth's parents, arrived in Rome, and the Fishers were their constant companions. At one point, Fisher alerted the press that the foursome would be dining in a local restaurant not far from the Associated Press headquarters. The diners were photographed in harmony while the rumors of Taylor-Burton still circulated around the world. That same week, Skouras prepared to fly to Rome to calm everyone down, and Louella Parsons carried a front-page story in the Los Angeles Herald-Examiner to the effect that the Fisher marriage was at last over. Fisher denied all vehemently.*]

■■■■■■■■■■■■■

Dear Nat,

I'm hoping Mank will show me a rough assembly of all the footage before I go. I have a $10 bet with Mank that he will get an Academy nomination for best director—he's sure he won't. He says he had two out of the five actresses nominated two years ago, Taylor and Hepburn for *Suddenly, Last Summer,* and he didn't get a nomination. Also, he gave me 20 to 10 that Bosley Crowther would rap it. We're in the process of negotiating what's a rap and what's not. He says anything less than Excellent in the *Variety* Box Score is a rap; I'll hold out for Good-Excellent.

Did I tell you that Otto Fuerbringer, *Time* Magazine's managing editor, was here and chatted with Mank? After a nice talk, Mank invited him out again, at which time Fuerbringer said, "I'm leaving tomorrow and it's either you or the Pope," to which Joe replied, "Well, at least the Pope's got a finished script."

Taylor-Fisher are lovey-dovey again, but I think it's phony. Especially since he never comes on set when Burton is working with her, and Burton-Taylor on set are so close you'd have to pour hot water on them to get them unstuck.

Jack Paar has cabled that he wants to film an interview with Taylor-Fisher for his show. Figures to be upbeat because Paar is always maligned by the press too and would want to be *the good guy* and *the hero* and be their friends (the Fishers). I'm sure the Fishers won't do it—if they remain the Fishers.

Love,
Jack

P.S. Big meeting at Grand Hotel yesterday: Mank, Skouras, WW, Merman, etc. After Mank leaves, a phone call comes from Levathes in Hollywood for Merman. Merman has a big argument with Levathes, ending up by saying, "Call him and tell him yourself." Skouras says, "What's up?" Merman tells him: "Pete says Joe is too slow and wants me to bite him." SPS calls Levathes back in Hollywood and tells him, "Call Joe, but tell him how great the footage is." So Levathes does this and Mank then calls SPS, saying, "Who told Levathes to call me?" Funny? Sad? That's our company. *J.*

■■■■■■■■■■■■

MARCH 20   BRODSKY   ROME
AWAITING APPROVAL STOP BIG BOYS STALLING MY DEPAR-
TURE STOP SKOURAS SAYS HANDS TIED STOP UNBELIEVABLE
BUT THEY DONT WANT SPEND MONEY MY PLANE TICKET
STOP PICTURE COST ONLY 25 MILLION AND THEY DONT
WANT TO SPEND SIX HUNDRED STOP CAN YOU GET WANGER
INTERVENE BEST WEISS

MARCH 21   WEISS   NEW YORK
WANGER WRITING SKOURAS STRONG LETTER URGING YOU
COME HERE REPLACE ME STOP BALLOON UP TODAY WITH
BOTH SYBIL EDDIE ON THE LOOSE WRITING LOVE JACK

■■■■■■■■■■■■

Dear Nat,

Sybil is leaving again, this time to take the kids to London and Eddie is bugging out. Up until now we have done a great job of keeping all the stuff in the right channels, but most of the dirty stories are going to bust wide open any day. It's unavoidable.

Paar didn't come, but Peggy Cass did and we're filming a 5-minute interview on the Forum with Richard Burton. In order to set this up, I got Piero Portalupi (our second unit cameraman who only happened to shoot the chariot scene from *Ben-Hur*) to film it. I also snagged Randy Macdougall [co-author with Mankiewicz and Sidney Buchman of the *Cleopatra* screenplay] to write-direct it and then got our editor, Dorothy Spencer, to agree to put it together. If it all works out, I should get a small Emmy or Oscar. At any rate, if it all works out, Paar will use it probably on his last show, Thursday. Please watch it and then send two cables. One saying: "Burton interview Paar show greatest plug picture has had all New York talking about fabulous break" so I can show it to all the people who helped. Then send me a separate cable telling me your real reaction. Thanks and love.

Jack

■ ■ ■ ■ ■ ■ ■ ■ ■ ■ ■ ■

MARCH 28   BRODSKY   ROME
BURTON INTERVIEW PAAR SHOW GREATEST PLUG PICTURE
HAS HAD ALL NEW YORK TALKING ABOUT FABULOUS BREAK
REGARDS WEISS

MARCH 28   BRODSKY   ROME
I LIKED IT LOVE WEISS

Dear Jack,

If we thought the place was berserk before, you should have seen it now that SPS has had all-day meetings with the top brass on the product shortage. We have no pictures for 1963, that's all. It seems that Levathes insists on not rushing pictures into release, something long talked about here, but never practiced; it accounts, among other things, for the fact *The Hustler* did less than it deserved. Therefore we won't have—he won't give them to us—*Mr. Hobbs Takes a Vacation* or *The Inspector* until late June or July. Not that they could bring in enough money if we did have them, but they could kid themselves into it. So, it's an emergency, we're desperate, we have nothing to release during the first part of May and June. The solution? Kill the intended "art" playoff on *Caligari* and go with it immediately (in May) on a "mass," "crash" basis. Maybe invest a lot of money in an ad campaign, and who knows, we may have another *Snow White and the Three Stooges* on our hands.

Two days ago SPS announced at a meeting that *Cleopatra* wouldn't be ready for release before March of 1963! Remember when it was to be in time for this year's annual stockholders' meeting?

My leaving still undecided.

> Love,
> *Nat*

●●●●●●●●●●●●●

MARCH 29   WEISS   NEW YORK
FISHER BOUNCED SYBIL FLYING BURTON TAYLOR GOING
OUT IN PUBLIC FOR FIRST TIME STOP GET UNDER THE DESK
STOP AM TERRIFIED STOP BRODSKY

MARCH 30   BRODSKY   ROME
PAPERS ARE FILLED TAYLOR BURTON ON TOWN STOP ANGRY
LETTERS POURING IN STOP EXECS UPSET BECAUSE AFFAIR
NOW PUBLIC THOUGHT YOU SHOULD KNOW WEISS

■■■■■■■■■■■■■

Dear Nat,

It gets more incredible every day. So many highlights, I don't know where to begin, so I'll just jot down the ones I remember.

1. Burton says to me, "Jack, love, I've had affairs before. How did I know the woman was so fucking famous? She knocks Khrushchev off the front page." So I say, "Rich, it's none of my business, but you can't very well deny everything in print and then go out on the Via Veneto till three in the morning." So he says, "I just got fed up with everyone telling us to be discreet. I said to Liz, 'Fuck it, let's go out to fucking Alfredo's and have some fucking fettuccine.'"

2. Meeting Emlyn Williams, who is Burton's friend and the emissary of his friends in England, here to stop Liz-Dickie. We spent an hour of hilarity, Williams, me, Burton, a *Life* reporter and photog here doing piece. Williams and Burton did great bits and Burton did hilarious imitation of Roddy McDowall-Rex Harrison fight, where Harrison, after being asked by McDowall to photograph him, says, "Well, you see, Roddy, that is, well, I'm sorry, but, well, the fact is . . . I just don't like you."

3. Taylor and me in a half-hour argument on "Eyewitness to History." CBS here wants to do a class documentary on the making of the film, not touching the personal mess. But Taylor says no. Her quote to me: "The picture has had too much fucking publicity." I tell her this will balance bad stuff and be great break. She argues, I argue. Guess who won? Anyway, I have Burton working on her. He feels it's important for her, but she said no to him the first time he tried her at my request. Now he tells me he thinks it's because she's afraid she can't really speak anything but written lines. He says he will coax her and tell her he'll write something for her. When I asked what about Mank, Burton bridled and said he'd do it, not Mank.

4. Up until a couple of days ago, everyone thought Burton was giving a great performance offstage. Now he seems like a different person, so caught up in Taylor's web. Anyway RB told JLM that "I fall more in love with her each day."

Love,
Jack

■■■■■■■■■■■■■

APRIL 1   BRODSKY   ROME
STOP ALREADY WITH THE PUBLICITY I KNOW YOUR FEEL-
INGS WERE HURT BUT ISNT THIS GOING TOO FAR STOP WE
ARE ON PAGE ONE OF DAILY NEWS AND MIRROR FOR FIVE
DAYS IN ROW STOP I THINK THATS BETTER THAN WORLD
WAR II STOP CONFIDENTIALLY EXECUTIVES VERY UNHAPPY
LOVE WEISS

Dear Nat,

It's an insane asylum here. Incredible day, incredible. Spent the whole day trying to get Taylor to make some kind of statement re Fisher in hospital. Got nothing. Guess I'm just as well off. Burton told WW at time of big mess, "Walter, I never thought it would come to this." Taylor told Burton she'd live in a cold-water flat to be with him. He said he wanted to go back to the Old Vic and she said she'd give up acting just to be out front. Enough. One explanation, and it sounds right to me, is that Burton told Sybil, "Look, this pic is important to me; go to England until this mess clears or until end of pic." This version has it that RB can out-maneuver ET. We'll see. I'd bet on her.

What a day! Earl Wilson woke me up at 5 A.M. calling from Beverly Hills to tell me about Eddie being in the hospital in New York. Also went through one of the most spectacular *Cleo* conversations yesterday with Elizabeth, Burton, Mank and Mank's son, Tom, in Mank's dressing-room trailer. Can you imagine a conversation where everyone starts putting Fisher down? After a while I begin to feel, "Maybe I'm wrong, maybe it was *his* fault." That's what she can do with those eyes of hers! Taylor turns to me and says, "Do you think Eddie will divorce me?" I began to feel sorry for her until I got out into the air.

Love,
Jack

■■■■■■■■■■■■

New York, April 4

Dear Jack,

All the execs here sit around every morning talking about how the romance will damage the *Cleo* boxoffice and only Charlie and I feel that everybody but everybody will go to see the pic to say that they can see on screen what's going on off it. Charlie has been telling them to sign Burton to a six-picture deal. But apparently M and M don't see it that way.

I'm surprised at Charlie backing us on the romance, after how nervous he was at *Francis of Assisi*. Remember when our star Brad Dillman, just divorced, wanted to bring Suzy Parker to the opening, and Charlie forbade it, saying "Saints come alone"?

Love,

Nat

P.S. Has it occurred to you that Rome is a kind of crazy Actors Studio with Taylor-Burton rehearsing off camera?

NW

55

■■■■■■■■■■■■

Dear Nat,

When Burton went to Paris the first time on *The Longest Day,* four weeks ago, they couldn't get anybody to interview him. Now, basking in the reflection of Miss Taylor's sex appeal, he *is* hot. This time it was another story. I had a phone call from Paris with the fill-in. Burton's arrival was covered by 40 photographers, newsmen, newsreel, etc. Sybil arrived, at a different airport, an hour earlier. The press got them together at the hotel. Burton looked very tired, but it was treated (by Sybil, at least) as a kind of "reunion." Luckily, Liz didn't go along.

Today—Sunday—the day they are shooting at the Paris studio, some 50 press people showed. All were clamoring for news and pictures, but they weren't allowed on set. Burton finally made a statement a few minutes ago in which he said Sybil was going to London when he goes back to Rome tonight, but she will join him there later. By the way, Sybil and Richard put the blame on us, while in Paris, for what's been going on here in Rome! Both said the publicity people weren't lifting a finger to publicize either the *Cleopatra* picture or any performer other than Elizabeth Taylor. Isn't that incredible?

Love,
Jack

P.S. I have just received a letter from Dick Brooks. [At this point, Brooks and Greg Morrison were Weiss's right-hand men in New York.] Let me quote some of it, because he's written that you weren't at the boardroom meeting after the screening of *Mr. Hobbs Takes a Vacation.*

Well, we're finished looking at *Hobbs* and Charlie tells us all to go into the boardroom for a meeting with Skouras. We go in and I am sitting at the far end of the table, cigarette in hand, legs crossed, head tilted back on chair. Skouras says, "You der."

I say, "Brooks, Mr. Skouras, Dick Brooks," like I was itching for a fight.

He says, "Dick, vat did you tink of de pitzah?"

I say, "Mr. Skouras, I think it is pretty good, but per-

56

haps if I was a father or grandfather I could relate to it better."

He says to Charlie, "Ver did you get a guy like that?"

Charlie says, "I guess he is a hardboiled newspaper-man."

SPS says, "I mean, Dick, vat do you think of it for money?"

I say, "It is a pretty good family picture, should do well and be very successful." He turns to the other people, some of whom are unenthusiastic, but most of the guys cackle and say it's great, and Michel says we should have had four more like it last year and we would have made money.

Skouras turns to me again and says, "You der," and I say, "Brooks, Mr. Skouras, Dick Brooks."

He says, "Dick, vould you have made the pitzah?"

"Yes," I say, "I would have made it." But, I am think-ing, not with that script and that director. Then SPS asks me if I ever read the Bible. I say yes.

"If you don't believe in Christianity, you can't sell Christianity, if you don't believe in Judaism, you can't sell Judaism," he says to Charlie. Then, "Charlie, I think it may be better if you take Dick off de assignment. He doesn't have de entoosiasm."

Charlie says, "He'll do the job."

I cut in at this point and in a hushed room of thirty people, I say the following: "Mr. Skouras, I have not been ecstatic about every picture Fox has produced."

He says, "I don't understand vat you are saying."

I say, "Mr. Skouras, I have never been overwhelmingly happy with every picture that Fox has produced."

He says, "That is understandable."

I say, "Mr. Skouras, I have never shirked a duty on my job for all the years that I have worked here. I have given my all in every job assigned me. My personal opinion of films never interferes with my job. Before I came here I worked for a man whose product could hardly be asso-ciated with the word *artistic*. But there too I never shirked a duty and I gave that product my all. And with

57

Mr. Hobbs I intend to give it my all in the same manner as other pictures."

Well, Jack, have you ever heard the words in your ears, like bouncing off the walls? The room is hushed and for about five long seconds there is silence. Skouras then tells some meager joke and the meeting breaks up. Charlie calls me down and I tell him that I am sorry if I embarrassed him. He says no. He says I should have said it was a swell picture for Mom and Dad and other bullshit. He says to me that I should bring the breaks on *Hobbs* down to Skouras and rub his nose in it.

It feels as if I'd never left.

Love,
Jack

■■■■■■■■■■■■

Dear Nat,

What can I tell you? The pressure is mounting and all of us feel it. Even Burton, usually the great guy, is now nervous, irritable, drinking. Shamroy predicts Burton will end up like John Barrymore. The other day, while shooting a small scene at the Forum, in which he has to ride horseback through a crowd (he can't ride and is frightened of the horse), Burton lost his temper at Shamroy and Mankiewicz for the first time. He screamed at them, in front of all, "Fuck off, can't you bastards get the fucking thing right once? Don't you know what bloody torture it is riding through this crowd?"

Roddy McDowall has moved out of the Burton villa, so uncomfortable is everything. He's moved into his own apartment in town, but is still friendly with the parties concerned.

Everyone here is very worried that Dorothy Kilgallen is getting all the scoops. Day after day her headlines read as if she were here!

The weather seems to be brightening and at long last we may get Taylor up on that Sphinx, if we can ever get her out of Burton's arms. During one of the love scenes the other day, Mankiewicz said, "Cut," then louder, *"Cut."* Then he said to them, "I feel as if I'm intruding!"

Love,
Jack

■ ■ ■ ■ ■ ■ ■ ■ ■ ■ ■ ■

APRIL 11   BRODSKY   ROME
GOT THE OK STOP ARRIVING APRIL 29 STOP EINFELD SAYS UP
TO ME CLEAN HOUSE AND GIVE TAYLOR NEW IMAGE STOP
THATS ALL LOVE NATHAN

■■■■■■■■■■■■

New York, April 13

Dear Jack,

Just got the final okay and will be there on April 29 as I cabled you. The current madness has involved the testimonial dinner to Skouras (last night at the Waldorf). Everyone mutters under his breath about what a perfect time this was for a dinner in view of everything that's happened. There was a hastily called sales meeting at which SPS said, "I would rather go to my own funeral than to the dinner for me tonight" and—pleadingly, "Why don't one of you boys come up here and put a knife through my heart? It would be kinder than to force me to go to that dinner." At the dinner itself, Papa was more subdued, less jovial than I have ever seen him at a gathering like this. One had to be touched by the predicament he is in. As we've said before, he *does* have such size and color— all too rare these days.

We've rewritten the annual report thirteen times and it finally goes to the printer over the weekend. It seems The Boat insists on printing the figures in more exact detail than before.

We saw *Lisa* [formerly *The Inspector*] yesterday. What can I say? You won't believe me if I tell you. All right, I'll tell you. Dolores Hart and Stephen Boyd getting on and off barges in Amsterdam canals. Philip Dunne, on whom we can always rely, has directed one of Fox's all-time stiffs. Charlie is readying an all-out sex campaign though, and if it doesn't save the picture, at least it'll probably get him investigated by some congressional committee.

Love,
Nat

■ ■ ■ ■ ■ ■ ■ ■ ■ ■ ■ ■

Dear Nat,

It's a good thing you've gotten the OK, because, baby or no, I would have to be rotated. In war you're only on the front lines for a few weeks, but this!

Yesterday morning, one of the Italian papers carried a blazing front-page story that it really wasn't Taylor and Burton at all. Mankiewicz, says the story, has ordered Burton to be seen with Taylor as a cover-up for the Mankiewicz-Taylor love affair. Burton, according to the story, is a "shuffle-footed idiot" who is forced to do his director's bidding.

On the set today, after the story was circulated and Taylor had laughed that high-pitched cackle of hers, Burton shuffle-footed over to Mankiewicz, rolled his eyes and said, "Duh, Mister Mankeawitz, sir, do I have to sleep with her again tonight?"

The AP forced me to ask Mank to comment on the story. I asked him, and do you know what the director of *All About Eve* and *A Letter to Three Wives*, my four-time Oscar winner, said? Of course you do, because it made headlines. He said, "The real story is that I'm in love with Richard Burton and Elizabeth Taylor is the cover-up for us." Whereupon he kissed Burton on the mouth and left. I called after him, asking whether he would give me something for AP, and he said to use that, so I did. I called AP and got a guy I didn't know and he took it all down faithfully. Then I called Dan Gilmore at UPI and gave it to him. As I was leaving the office, Gilmore called and said, "I'm just checking, Jack. I think I know your voice, but was that you on the phone just now? I have to be sure on this one." When I got back to the apartment, a friend from AP called and said the man I'd given the story to didn't speak English too well and the boys there couldn't believe he'd gotten the message straight!

Love,
Jack

■■■■■■■■■■■■

APRIL 16   WEISS   NEW YORK
WENT BOWLING WITH REX HARRISON LAST NIGHT STOP
THOUGHT THAT WORTH A CABLE LOVE JACK

■■■■■■■■■■■■

New York, April 17

Dear Jack,

I have my instructions from Skouras. Upon getting to Rome, I am to change the public image. I am to convince you and Wanger that Taylor must not go out at night, she and Burton must not be seen together, she is to stay at home and study her lines for the next day. When I asked him if it would help for me to carry his words directly from him to her, he nervously said, "Don't talk to her. No, no, don't talk to her. Just tell Wanger and Brodsky, that's all." He wants me to bring all the mounting evidence of public and press scorn for Taylor and Burton, as proof that the American public will boycott the film. Not the actual clips, which I told him have been sent, but typed-up extracts. When I suggested that maybe the word of Skouras to Taylor would mean more to her, he admitted with a certain sadness that unfortunately it would not help at all, that Wanger is the only person who might influence her.

Love,
Nat

P.S. Did I tell you some of Groucho Marx's great lines at the SPS testimonial last week? "Mr. Skouras is president of a company dedicated to good picture making and some very peculiar bookkeeping." "Mr. Skouras has never made a horror film intentionally." He concluded with "Mr. Skouras faces the future with courage, determination and terror."

NW

Rome, April 20

Dear Nat,

Maybe Groucho Marx should be president!

When I told Wanger that the execs are all upset over what's been going on, he cracked, "What the hell do you expect from guys who've lost 70 million in the past few years?" Nat, my best reaction is from people who come here and see the shooting—celebrities, actors, directors, exhibitors, tourists; people like Gilbert Miller, John Steinbeck, Walter Lippmann. To a man they are all absolutely dying to see *Cleo*, thrilled by what they see here, excited by the gossip. The public may call Taylor names, but they can't wait to see her. Wanger made a good point about all the *tsouris*. Ingrid Bergman was a saint to all her fans when Wanger had her in *Joan of Arc* and when she got in trouble she cracked and destroyed that image. Taylor is the exact opposite, that is her principal attraction, and when she's playing Cleopatra, there should be no trouble. Anyway, Wanger is writing (I'm the ghost writer) to Skouras: a nice long, long letter detailing all the covering up and sleepless nights we've had, a compendium of all the machinations of running this type of operation. I hope that will help. Christ, this film is a national institution now and has just served to whet the appetites of editors for material on the film. And, of course, we have had an enormous amount of positive publicity, too.

Love,
Jack

■■■■■■■■■■■■

New York, April 20

Dear Jack,

To sum up what is going on in New York and what you will find here on your return: SPS knows his days are numbered, but he's fighting desperately to have a hand in naming his successor. He's about given up on having *Cleo* ready in time to save his presidency, and while he may not step down at the stockholders' meeting next month, it can't be long in coming. I hope we don't end up at the mercy of a Levathes or some lightweight. The department is functioning well; the boys are the best, you know that. As for Charlie and all the infighting, I can only wish you good fortune. Probably by the time you get this, our bags will be packed and we'll be ready. The thought of flying has me terrified, but then so does the vision of stepping into the Taylor-Burton mélange. You've done nobly and deserve your rotation. See you soon.

Love,
Nat

■■■■■■■■■■■■■

APRIL 21   WEISS   NEW YORK
BURTON TAYLOR GONE FOR WEEKEND WITH PRESS IN HOT
PURSUIT STOP WHO KNOWS WHEN THEYLL BE BACK STOP
STANDING BY FOR HURRICANE BECAUSE STRONGLY BELIEVE
SYBIL ON WAY BACK AND SHE DOESNT KNOW THEYRE GONE
LOVE JACK

■■■■■■■■■■■■

Rome, April 22

Dear Nat,

By now you've seen the papers on the wild weekend. On Sunday, all the papers and wire services were calling, asking me to comment on the two of them shacked up at Porto San Stefano. Then WW calls and tells me that Sybil is on her way back and he has to tell Liz and Rich. Do you know how we called them? I had to get the number from UPI! Then I gave it to Wanger and he called. But it was too late, they had apparently had a tiff and came back separately.

Love,
Jack

68

■■■■■■■■■■■■

Rome, *April 23*

Dear Nat,

To close out my writing from Rome, you ought to have a rundown on the people in the department who handle our Italian publicity. Nella, helpful and capable, worked on *Ben-Hur*. Nanni, her diminutive writer, is a nice guy, who is ashamed, I think, to be working on *Cleo*. They're both wonderful, marvelously funny, and I think they may hold the key to the *paparazzi* problem.

I have come to learn who the *paparazzi* are. Remember that horde of photographers who followed Ekberg everywhere in *La Dolce Vita?* Well, they're for real. They are as numerous as termites and they multiply the same way. They are trying to take candids of Liz and Burton wherever they can. We discovered one with a camera in his tie in the commissary yesterday! One of them —the current "king of the *paparazzi*"—sidled up to me on the Via Veneto yesterday, asking me to steal a negative for him, any negative of Liz. He told me if he could claim he took it—it didn't even have to be compromising—he could make us both a lot of money. Burton told me that they've been following him, trying to provoke him into a fight, so that he'd take a poke at one of them and someone would get a shot worth thousands of lire. You'll enjoy them.

Erna Stenbuck, Joe Mankiewicz' sister, has been doing translations of the Italian copy, among other things. She's worked in Italy for ten years or so and really knows the ropes. Just don't say anything bad about Mank in front of her. Loyal. And her brother's sister. Nanni claims he found her writing in a piece of copy, *"Cleopatra*, directed by my brother, Joseph L. Mankiewicz."

This will reach you either Friday or Saturday, I imagine. We will be at the airport to usher you in with singing, Chianti and laughter at 7:40 A.M. I have sent Sam home and my mother and father met him at the airport. This looks like a terrible week, but I imagine yours will be as rough.

Thanks for all the marvelous letters, the information on Fox and what I'll find. It should be an interesting switch and I'm especially looking forward to your telling Taylor and Burton to stop seeing each other.

Love, finally, from Rome.

JB

■■■■■■■■■■■■■

PART TWO

■■■■■■■■■■■■

PART TWO

[*Excerpt from Weiss's notebook*]
Notes to myself, one eye on posterity:

Golda and I arrived, bleary, Sunday morning. Good old Alitalia. Jack and Dorothy met us at the airport. Can Jack really speak Italian, or is he just a good mimic? He seemed able at least to cope with the porters; maybe he can just count in Italian. Now it is four days later and after the world's quickest indoctrination, they have left to spend a week in London on the way back to New York. I better recap the highlights of the four days we spent together.

1) The night Jack and I spent in Wanger's suite with Mankiewicz and then at dinner with Wanger at the Grand, with Eleanor Parker dropping by. The theory evolved of Elizabeth as one of the least promiscuous of women, because she intends to marry each man she falls in love with—and does. Each, for the time, is Prince Charming. It's very schoolgirlish, actually, to pledge undying love with each. It's also an interesting theme for a play.

2) It was damned nice of Walter and Joe to be so warm and hospitable to us. Joe holed up in the hotel, working nights and weekends on script, never ruffled. He seemed even more relaxed than a year ago when we discussed that brilliant treatment of *Justine* he was writing in his town house in New York. They do hang on every word of the blow-by-blow Fox battle I could recount. It has been quite a winter and you can see more clearly every day how the climaxing crisis of Fox is interlocked with what *Cleopatra* will finally be. That Mank can be that calm, puffing on his pipe and regaling us with his Hollywood psychoanalysis (Wanger is no slouch either) while the company is going so crazy they are applying the screws to the one man who can save them—they just don't understand—is really breath-taking. I thought Jack and I were pretty clever, but it was really Wanger who managed it, to convince Joe to let us see the assembled film. Nobody from the cast has seen it. Even Joe hasn't seen it all at once. But Jack is leaving and can go back to propagandize. I am arriving and don't know where to begin, and this at least will bring me right up to date on the only thing that finally counts—the film itself. Also I think from the beginning of the year or two we have known each other

a little, Mank and WW realize we do speak the same language. So it is agreed, we are to see the film.

3) My reaction, shared by Jack. The first few minutes you can't quite adjust: there it is on the screen. All the talk that she hasn't worked and that it's not even half-finished, not true. We walk across Cinecittà, from that awful company shack that is our office to the small white building which houses the screening room. There are six or eight rows of comfortable seats. Walter presses the button and they start. It is *Cleopatra*, some four and a half hours of it on the screen, not close-cut but cut for continuity.

It has universality, majesty and wit. Like all legitimate theater it begins with the spoken word. Nothing has ever been written at this level for the screen. It is Shakespeare and Shaw for our time; Joe has found a contemporary language which is neither colloquial, which would be silly, nor too stately, which would be antique. The spectacle is tasteful. She responds in some instinctive way to Joe, as years ago she did to George Stevens in A *Place in the Sun*. Burton is the actor of his generation, or at least is with Paul Scofield. Harrison, if anything, is better than Burton. Roddy McD. is like a fourth star, a brilliant coldness as Octavian. In the end this is all that counts; it is art finally that must be served, and if we can do anything to help Mank and WW in that cause now that the howling dogs are in full pursuit, then there will have been some purpose to our being here after all.

Obviously Joe does not know what he has, or he could not really believe as he seems to that the critics are going to demolish the picture. In part because it's from an American director, hence suspect; in part because of the notoriety that has cheapened the image of a serious work; and in part because the critics, like public scolds, as Joe says, will take a prudish position because of their (hypocritical) outraged morality. I think Joe is wrong. The film is both scholarly and showmanly, no mean achievement.

4) I'm glad that Jack was still here when Sheilah Graham arrived. She has always been very good to us. I still melt when she tells me some of her "Scott reminiscences." She's one hell of a reporter, and she knows the story is here. She also knows there isn't much we can do about it. Everybody's double-talking her; they don't want to see her (Taylor just won't), but they are afraid not to. I don't know yet how we will resolve it but I am seeing "in

small" what the press game here is all about—that and the business of the press phoning all night long to find out, or report, that Taylor and Burton have been seen here—or there. Who cares?

5) A word about Rome. This is—what—the fourth time Golda and I have been here, but the first time that it is to be for a long time, relatively, and we are not here as tourists. Except that we are eating at the Roman and not the tourist places—and they are so much better—the best is little Mimmo's place, Flavia's, I haven't seen Rome. I see the Hotel de la Ville early and late, we have a balcony with a view of the Spanish steps, I walk down them—and they are now beautifully bedecked with flowers during the Easter season—each morning to meet the car which is to take me out the Appia Antica to Cinecittà and it deposits me back at the hotel twelve hours later with just time to change, to eat and to bed. Maybe it will change—for the better. For now Rome is Flavia's. The story of how everybody knew it to be the "official" *Cleopatra* restaurant catering all his food to Mank at the hotel and to Taylor and Burton at their villas on the Old Appian Way, and how outraged poor Mimmo was when it was reported she was sick from "food poisoning" because everyone knew where the food came from, is delicious—like his food, come to think of it. Jack tells me the story they gave out originally said "baked beans" caused the illness, but after Mimmo protested it was changed to "American baked beans" and blamed on the contents of a can.

6) Finally, I think, for these interim notes, and then I had better hold off until after the weekend when I can write Jack: the first meeting. Jack took me yesterday to the stars' "dormitory." There hasn't been any shooting this week because of the "accident" after the weekend at Porto San Stefano, so Elizabeth wasn't working, but we phoned over and they said Richard was in. So we strolled over, so that Jack could introduce me to him at least before he left, and for him to say goodbye. We went up to Burton's dressing room, the door was open, we looked in and saw he wasn't there but we could hear the shower going in the adjoining room. We stepped back, out into the corridor, to wait for Burton to finish when a cute blonde suddenly brushed by us to go into Burton's room. Jack did a double-take and said to her, "It's you." I was confused for an instant and then realized it was indeed Elizabeth —but in a blond wig. After all I had met her only once before, in

New York a year ago. She whispered to us not to let on, invited us in to his room and then the three of us waited for him to emerge so that she could surprise him. She called out to him—presumably so that he might not surprise us—that she was waiting and that Jack "and a friend" (me) were with her. I don't know what the hell our conversation was, but I'll never forget the deep suntan, the orange dress with to all appearances nothing of consequence beneath it—nothing that is but Elizabeth—and that incongruous Sybil-like blond wig she was suddenly affecting. The first words I heard were Richard's as he emerged from the bath, and they were not addressed to Jack and me. "How much do you charge?" he asked. The necessary things were said, and Jack and I left fairly soon, closing the door behind us.

Dear Jack,

Who can wait? I'll send this off today so that it ought to be at home waiting for you when you return on Thursday. My first and most important jotting is simply this: How could you? I know, I know, you warned me. How could I complain so about the work in New York when even drumming up some trade for *Caligari* at the Paramount Theater is less degrading and has more integrity than trying to suppress the confessions of their Italian maid who has threatened to tell all. This is the lowest point on the human scale I've ever been associated with.

You remember our meeting Sheilah at the airport last week. She knew damn well Burton didn't plan to see her. After you left, it looked as though he would, then it turned out Sheilah was being tricked (not by me, needless to say). She made it clear to me just how enraged she was, and rightly so. The upshot was that Roddy finally got Richard to change his mind and consent to see Sheilah.

I suppose Burton deserves a medal for performance. Once the meeting was set, in a private curtained alcove behind the big lounge at the Grand (I brought Sheilah there and I don't think either of us really believed Burton was going to show, but he did and on time), he came through. He gave Sheilah 90 minutes of intellect, wit, charm, brilliance and sex—the last of course only by radiation. Her theme was that *Cleopatra* and the romance, by design or not, had upped his market price for his coming projects. He went into them, particularly the Sartre project, with a condescending attitude, faintly that of "the poor dear doesn't really know who Sartre is." Also as though he thought his vocabulary was a little too much for her, and she did say she wanted to quote him exactly, he slowed down his torrent of words to carefully spell out d-i-l-a-t-o-r-y for her. He can be cruel. He told her that a friend, he wouldn't say who, had cabled him: *Do you want your name to be that of a great actor or merely a household word?* He didn't say who it was, only in quoting the cable he imitated the actor who actually had sent it. It was one of the great samples of mimicry one will ever hear, and I started to say "It's Olivier," but by now Sheilah was as rattled as I was in trying to keep up with his mercurial changes of pace. "Who do you mean?" she asked.

"Gielgud? Coward? Oh, no, I promised not to ask." And he never told her, racing on to another subject. You can imagine how Burton handled the key questions—"just friends"—and Sheilah must realize he was lying in his teeth to her, so blatantly that my eyes popped. But Sheilah seems to have gone away happy; after all she does have the one full-bodied interview either of them has given. It will make juicy copy.

The interview was one of the moments that make up for it; but there is too much to be made up for and not enough moments like that.

Later that night, or rather at 2:30 A.M. in the morning, I was wakened out of the first sleep I've had in Rome with news that *Gente* [the Italian magazine] is bringing out the maid's story and a panicky voice saying that UPI is carrying a report on it to New York. Wanger wants to sue. Sue? But isn't the maid's story true? I tried to get the office on the phone, but it was then ten in the evening at home, you're in London, and the operator at the Hotel de la Ville keeps clicking off the phone, saying in all the English he can muster, "You've completed your call? Good night," and I'm screaming that I haven't even gotten the number yet—and I hate Italy, and *Cleopatra*, and you for getting me into this in the first place. Next day the crisis seems to have evaporated some; really it's like worrying about *Confidential* all the time. It's all so petty. Maybe nobody gives a damn outside Italy.

Later that night

We got the word. Tomorrow is *Der Tag*. I tried to reach you by phone in London, but couldn't. The weather looks good, and it looks like tomorrow they will shoot the rest of the Procession. We shall miss you. Shamroy can't believe you are gone. I called and invited Arnaldo Cortesi at the *Times*. He was very flattered and said he wishes he could come himself, but he would send a man; that Skouras will be here also pleased him, the man he is sending is Greek, and could I introduce him to Skouras?

So tomorrow with 40 press out for the big day—including the wire services and the *Times* and the *News* and the *Herald Tribune* —I have to cut out at 2:30 to go to the airport to meet Skouras and Moskowitz, the only ones coming, it seems. No explanation yet why Charlie is staying in Paris. A fun day coming up. But to-day somehow working at high gear I enjoyed myself.

In just over a week's time I do seem to have settled down, and I anticipate less trouble (maybe some) than when you left here a few days ago. The schedule now shows Ischia May 28 and Egypt July 1, so our goose is cooked until August 1 I'm sure, not even counting vacation. On the brighter side we *may* get into an apart-ment we have sublet (from a friend of a friend of Wanger's) by May 15 instead of May 20, which would be a blessing. The short weekend was most enjoyable, including the Roman Forum—from the Palatine top—as I'd never seen it before, glorious. Hot sun and beauty of summer came to Italy the past few days; actually got sunburned on the terrace of our hotel suite Sunday afternoon.

Thanks for everything—the welcome, the friendship, the gin, and the advice, all of the highest order. Maybe years from now we will look back upon the whole thing as having been enriching. This had better stop now and I'll mail it in the morning. Hope you and Dorothy—Dorothy and you really, as she's the one who doesn't want to fly—had a pleasant trip home and are loving being there.

Nathan

[A *phone call from Brodsky in London to Weiss in Rome*]

BRODSKY: How's it going?

WEISS: Frantic. I wrote you yesterday, and a letter will be waiting for you at home tomorrow or Thursday. I can't really talk now. We're doing it today, the Procession.

BRODSKY: You mean it? I waited seven months for it and they wait until I leave to shoot it. Who's out for it?

WEISS: Only half of Rome. Wanger has the cream of Roman society sitting out in the hot sun on a platform behind the camera, under parasols. I think they think they're here to watch Christians thrown to lions. Also any celebrities in town. And friends. Oh, it's a big day.

BRODSKY: Any press?

WEISS: Only *The New York Times*. They sent a Greek who wants to meet Skouras. I don't know if I should let him.

BRODSKY: Really?

WEISS: And the *Herald Trib*, the *News*, AP, UPI, Reuters. I think Tass is coming.

BRODSKY: Is Skouras there?

WEISS: Not yet. I'm going out to pick him and Moskowitz up at the airport this afternoon.

BRODSKY: While the Procession is being shot?

WEISS: What can I do?

BRODSKY: That's crazy.

WEISS: I sort of knew that, Jack, thanks. But Charlie called from Paris. He wants us to con Skouras into sending for him. He says he and some others were dropped in Paris to save "carfare"; it's just like at home. I have to go now.

BRODSKY: Wait. How do you like it? Any questions? Any problems?

WEISS: I vary every minute. Yes, it's exciting. And yes, it's an experience. And yes, there are moments that make up for a lot—I wrote you some of it. But basically this is the worst phase of all movie publicity. It's so degrading. You are really a servant for these people, pandering to all their whims. Maybe it's just this picture. These stars. But this is the way it must have been in the old days when there really were stars. I've got to go.

BRODSKY: Try to be of good cheer. And remember the cables are working. And pick up the phone. Give everybody my love.

WEISS: Goodbye, Jack.

Rome, May 9

Dear Jack,

I can't wait to write, even though we talked yesterday and obviously you will get this on the heels of the letter waiting for you at home already. But yesterday was really too much. That vast set, Rome in all its grandeur, thousands and thousands of everything—people, animals, props, you name it; and the Sphinx being hauled under the arch to Caesar's feet, and then our girl Liz a little shakily descending that golden staircase that tongues out of the Sphinx. With Joe sweating and screaming from his crane, while Roman society 1962 fans itself from that grandstand behind the cameras and the whole world seems to be going mad. I only saw some of it; of course it's a travesty that I have to cut out at the height of the biggest filming ever, with 40 or 50 press people on hand, to go to the airport. But cut out I do, eating a sandwich with crumbs flying in the car racing to the airport. Got there at 2:35, and in a minute there was Joe the Mosk come to do battle with Joe the Mank. There was someone from the Fox home office in Rome to arrange for the bags and with tip money. And then Papa, looking worse than death, never saw anything like it. He embraced me, said *Come sta* and I came back with the *Molto bene* and we were off: the man with baggage in one car, the rest of us in our car, headed for the studio.

The trip starts in silence. I break it. "Where is Charlie, Mr. Skouras?" I ask. "Is he coming on the next plane?" Silence.

Who finally breaks the silence (Skouras up front with Mario, the driver; me and Mosk on the back seat) but Joe: with a civil, friendly, human response like "He's not coming."

I then went into my routine, we have so many problems to resolve, we need him here, how is it he's not coming, etc. Stony silence from SPS, and embarrassed non-answers from Joe. Then SPS and Mosk get on what happened last week to Liz, how many more key scenes, how much longer, and all that. Then we got on to Sheilah and I went into a long recitation. Skouras came to on the point that all this wouldn't have started if someone had been able to tell Liz how to act to Sheilah last October. To which the reply was: "We are still looking everywhere for that someone

82

who will tell Elizabeth what to do. Do you have any idea who it may be?" SPS fell silent again.

We arrive on the set, SPS comes back to life, I get Bob, pix are taken of SPS and JM with Mank, Wanger, Liz, Burton, etc. I introduce SPS to the *Times* man, to Packard, to the UPI girl. He charms them all—the *Times* man being Greek yet. But I've missed all the great shots and Golda and Sheila Penn have had the time of their lives. Golda told me that while I was gone she shared a chair with Mrs. Taylor, Elizabeth's mother, who confided, "Elizabeth has asked us to stay!"

Suddenly in the midst of the next big shot, SPS and Mosk begin to depart with Wanger, and getting into the back seat SPS asks me have I seen the film? I say no, tho' Wanger hears me lie, so SPS says to Walter, "I would like to have Nat see the picture with me," and Wanger says, "Nat is a valued member of the firm, I'd love him to." So of course how can I refuse and say I don't want to or I saw it last week?

As the lights dimmed, SPS asked me to punch him if he starts to fall asleep, as he had not slept at all the night before. Almost at once SPS fell asleep. The first of the first three times I punched him, he shook my hand gratefully, the other two he was cordial. The fourth time he fell asleep he was angry that I woke him, but he explained he had seen this part of the film the last time he was in Rome. The fifth and sixth times I woke him it was because he started to snore, and on the fifth time he could be heard through the room and heads turned. The seventh time he roused out of sleep he cried out with meaningless gibberish as one does when roused in mid-sleep at night. The eighth, ninth and tenth times I woke him he seemed appreciative as 1) he had not seen the scene before; 2) he wanted to call his doctor as he wasn't feeling well; and 3) he had to go to the john, and left the proj. room exactly at the time of the Taylor bed-cutting scene, which then had to be run over for him at nine o'clock in the evening, when we all staggered out.

The president of the company fighting for its life and with $35 million at stake, so ill and tired as to sleep through *Cleopatra*, will remain one of my most vivid experiences. I on the other hand was all keyed up and could experience the film more fully than last time, and I must tell you I thought it better than I did the first time. Truly great. During the intermission, Joe Mosk said to me the picture is "wonderful"; throughout our being together he was warm, friendly, cordial, civil, and what's more at one point *personal.* He asked me, "How do you like it so far?" And we even talked about where I'm living, etc. Can you explain it? Can you believe it?

The basic thing the mission here by SPS and Mosk was supposed to accomplish, I suppose, is to get Mank to wrap up the picture now, close it down with the bare minimum of scenes for story continuity and scotch the rest of it. Maybe not even to save the rest of the money (they say none is left), so much as to be able to quell the rising Wall Street storm by announcing, "The picture is finished. Now we can start getting our money back." But it's not.

The next morning, taking SPS to the airport, he said he'd like Charlie to see the picture! (So why not bring him in the first place?) But to wait until he returned to Paris (a matter of a couple of hours), then get Wanger to cable him in Paris—after Wanger checks with Mank—saying that he, Wanger, suggests that Charlie come to Rome to see *Cleopatra.* Have been urgently trying to phone Charlie—in London for the day today (on *Rama,* I guess)—to tell him that this is in the works and that it looks like he'll come to Rome Thursday or Friday after all.

All the best,
n.

84

New York, May 13

Dear Nat,

It's Sunday night, first chance I've had to write, and even though I've got to change the ribbon on this machine tomorrow at the latest, if I don't write this now I won't get the chance tomorrow, I know.

Your two letters arrived yesterday. I enjoyed them both immensely, especially the SPS experiences. I hope by now things have shaken down into something resembling a life and that the time will pass quickly. . . .

Got sensational greeting at the office, everyone coming out of the bins and offices and hugging and kissing and hand shaking. (I don't trust them; what do they want?) No kidding, I was touched and moved and thrilled. They had recorded music set to go as I entered, flags in your (my temporary) office and banners, etc. What a welcome!

Everyone, the grocer, our next-door neighbors, ask, "Tell me, is it true about Taylor and Burton?" They all ask with smiles; no one really has an ax out for her, although she's not popular. But the public air about the thing is one of curiosity and amusement and excitement, not indignation. And when the fruit man asks me, "When is that movie coming out?" I think the penetration is fabulous.

I felt awful that we only had the four fastest days ever and never enough time to have the kind of talks we needed. I feel almost as if we still haven't seen each other. But we will again and this time, God willing, without the hectic quality of those four days.

Dorothy is so glad to be home she's blooming. She went to an eye doctor here, who explained her blurred vision as three Italian doctors and one obstetrician could not: it is common in 15% of pregnant women and will disappear when the baby comes. What a country! So we're back, you're there and we wish you love and a relaxed good time and success and fun. Much love,

Jack

Rome, May 13

Dear Jack,

I don't know where to start. First, I guess it's no secret any more that basically I hate it here.

You can't quite overcome the local attitude and viewpoint. You spend half your time warding off the local press. You know, Italy is simply not important for publicity on this film, because every Italian will go to see it anyway. That's why it's silly now to waste any time or material on the Italian market . . . but try to convince Nella and Nanni. They are great. I guess it's wonderful that they think Italy's so important. It must help every other picture that's made here.

Another topic, please. Well, we got Charlie here via the ruse, working on Skouras, etc. By the by, once the OK came from SPS, I got Charlie on the phone to tell him it worked and, sure enough, Charlie said he doesn't want to come to Rome just to see the picture! But he did—for just 24 hours. His single theme was that he didn't want to come here. He even said it to Wanger at the very moment Wanger was saying to him, "Well, it worked, I did what you wanted, I got you here." Charlie was annoyed that Walter hadn't come out to meet him at the plane. We had two hours of wrangling over lunch at the commissary before the screening— though after he said he didn't want to see anybody we offered to take him elsewhere for lunch. The wrangling centered on Sheilah Graham and how she had been mishandled by us, on why we're not close enough to Taylor to control her and force her to see Sheilah!

Then the screening. I saw some of it this time, my third time around in a couple of weeks. Charlie's enthusiasm was considerable though a little restrained; he feels it may eventually get its money back, and you know maybe that isn't too unshrewd a guess. At least Charlie was alive to it, and not, like Skouras, in a semi-asleep state.

Walter came over to Charlie at lunch, presupposing he would have dinner with him that night. I angered Charlie by telling WW we had looked into his office first but he wasn't there. Charlie quickly explained he just went up there to use the can as he figured it would be a clean one, no mean trick at Cinecittà. To the dinner overture, Charlie brusquely declined, saying he had a date. Late that night Charlie called Mank to tell him how wonderful he thought the picture was, but he never called Wanger, who remarked on it to me the next day—"The son of a bitch never even called to thank me for getting him here." As usual, Walter is right to the point. And I can sit in his office for hours (if I had them) shmoosing about the old days and what it was like with Hedy Lamarr on *Algiers*.

It's now May 14
(never got to mail the above last night)

Wanger has had me do six rewrites on the cable he's sending SPS for the annual stockholders' meeting tomorrow. He won't send SPS what SPS asked him for when he was here—that the key death scene is nearly finished and then, come what may, we have the picture—because Walter knows this could later be used against him if for some reason it never gets done. Walter says he's been asked to send so many different messages to the meeting to appease the stockholders that he's thinking of just sending: *Dear Spyros Will do our level best to carry out your contradictory instructions.*

Wanger also wants to give Skouras hell for his idea of showing some of the *Cleopatra* footage they got into New York from Pete L. on the Coast—in CinemaScope yet—to the stockholders tomorrow. This is foolish; talk about destroying an image! I told Walter what he should say to SPS, but Walter would like to accomplish it through Charlie. So I called Charlie, by now back in Paris, but Charlie agrees with SPS it should be shown; so that's that.

Mank had asked Wanger why I haven't been around to see him. I've been working, that's why. So I did stop by the set this morning. Mank wanted to know if I thought Charlie was telling him the truth about liking the film, and when I said I was sure he had been, Mank observed that Charlie for so long has had to say so many pictures are good which were truly terrible, he may not any longer know the difference. Joe is also convinced that the SPS trip here was just to get them to say the picture is finished when it's not, and Joe feels it would be a disservice to the picture and the stockholders to say it is.

We were having this conversation between bits and pieces of

87

Taylor. She interrupted to say he was keeping her waiting. He told her we were thinking up some ideas to get some publicity for the picture. She gave that her big, vulgar, mirthless laugh.

I suggested to her that we were going to send her on a tour of all the RKO neighborhood theaters during the three nights before the picture opens, and she threw back her head, laughed, and for a minute I thought she was going to come up with her "crazy," only she didn't. Joe went back to work, Liz went back to her scene (she does turn it on with a no-nonsense when those cameras go), which called for her to fall upon her knees on a pillow before the fire in which she sees the vision of Caesar's assassination. Before the take started, going down on her knees, she said to Joe, "You didn't think I could sink this low." Why does everything she says sound like *double entendre?*

I had better close this off soon. Not without telling you, while I was out at the set, Rex Harrison came around and asked to meet me; he has barely worked, of course, since you left, so he's not been around. Damn.

Must tell you today's terrace lunch story. By the way, now that the weather's better Taylor and Burton adorn the terrace almost daily, and it seems to be a great attraction for everybody. If the public which waits at the Cinecittà gate knew that the restaurant is open to them at all times from the side entrance, it might be worth buying into the restaurant.

At any rate I had the Burton cover story issue of *American Weekly* to show Richard, so I trotted on over and they invited me to join them. Almost at once Burton was admiring his picture and deep into the story on him in AW. I began to talk to Elizabeth about Bert Stern, who would love to come over toward the end of the month, and we'd get something new on the picture to plant in the big magazines later on—nearer to the time of the picture's release. She said, "Well, we'll be in Ischia by then," and I said, "Yes, that might give Bert the fresh background he'd like." So she said she'd love to have him—a pleasant switch from their being negative on all photographers and death on all press as "dangerous"—and then prodding Richard, she added, "Don't you agree?" and he roused himself out of self-admiration to say, "Don't I agree with what?" and she said, "Would we like Bert Stern to come with us to Ischia?" and Burton said, "Oh, yes, we'd love him to." So she

88

smiled and said, "OK, that's it." Now I heard a very perceptive observation on this: where you used to go to Eddie Fisher (a boy) and then he would ask Elizabeth do-we-want-such-and-such, now you go to Elizabeth directly and she asks Burton (a man) do-we-want-such-and-such. It's a contrast which does spell out the whole affair.

I don't know which way to end this: you may have detected I'm getting to like Rome, not *wild* about it, but liking it. Or: I had to undergo 60 minutes of torture in a dentist's chair—but facing a window overlooking the Spanish steps covered now with the sun-streamed flowers. But don't get me wrong—I hate Rome; I love Rome; I can't decide.

Love,
Nathan

■■■■■■■■■■■■

New York, May 17

Dear Nat,

I'm stopping everything tonight to try to get some of the things that I have been carrying around in my head down on paper. The press coverage on the meeting was so complete that the tear sheets sent you from the office really tell all. I phoned you, of course, but the connection was so poor I guess nothing got through other than that Skouras was kept in.

The implication was quite strong at the meeting that the picture was "in the bag" and nothing more to worry about, because they damn near had the one remaining "must" in the can—namely the girl's death, without which you can't very well end the story of *Cleopatra*. I know how this will assault everybody on your end. And the way the press is playing it up I'm worried that this could drive her off again, and then we'll really be in trouble. Even though Wanger never sent the kind of wire SPS wanted for the meeting, I'm afraid the net result is about the same it would have been if he did.

Greg is at the house for dinner, and I'll put him on with some observations he wants to make about the stockholders' meeting:

> Well, the mishmash and hodgepodge of "I have only one life to give for my company" and "Never have so few done so little" is over for another year, and the status quo is even more stationary than ever. You've probably seen the *Times* and *Trib* reports on the Greatest Little Show on Earth so I won't go into detail. Contrary to the other privates in this insanest of armies I beat the heat and the crush by perching on a stool in the projection room. As I peeped out of my 8 x 10 vantage point at the lineup across the front table, I was actually tempted to just start screaming at the crew who run this jernt. 'Twas really an amazing exercise in self-control not to blurt out all of the questions that any one of us could have asked to upend the party. In this case discretion was the better part of the weekly pay check and I abstained.
>
> Operating something like a grade-school outing, the holders of stock joyfully paraded in, were shown the way

to the restrooms and water fountains, wafted on a river of Greek tears, exposed to the euphorias awaiting the nation's moviegoers, given the old town meeting opportunity to question whether this trip has been necessary. Satisfied that they are in the best of all possible worlds, though unhappy about the lack of box lunches, this mass of mentality, whose little lives are rounded out to the last decimal point, trundled out into West 56 Street completely satisfied that they have come, seen and conquered.

Enough of this yearly medicine man show. Must say it was a saddening experience, not just witnessing Papa, the Aristotelian tragic hero, nearly plummet from power like a winged duck, but to take a big fat CinemaScope look at the gentlemen lined up across the table who draw down Gawd knows how many beans per annum. Christ, I'm making myself ill.

Sing a song of sixpence, a pocket full of wry schemes.

Question: Do you work for a large corporation? Is this a successful organization? . . . What? You lost how many beans last year? . . . Sorry, the panel is stumped. . . . There can be no company still operating with a deficit like that.

So keep gladiating, while I try to quiet Charlie who says our flicks are no longer arriving courtesy rubber heels, but are tipping in via bare feet. Many regards to you and yours from the tormented, mumbling New York stringer. And now, here's Jack.

It's Brodsky again. Basically Skouras told the stockholders that there would be a "major change" and that he's going to the studio with Rosenman to study it and will then make a recommendation to the board to effect "the change." All of us feel that this means elimination of the studio. His statement seemed to pacify the stockholders.

An elderly Jewish man, talking to Skouras, told him he knew of properties, things that were stage hits in the 'twenties, that would cost Fox "peanuts" and could be made cheaply. He listed titles like "The Quaker Girl" and "Damaged Goods." I was afraid Skouras would say to the guy, "Those are the pictures I want to make, but they won't let me." I thought that stockholder summed it up best though when he said to SPS, "Listen, we're paying you good money, so you better produce. If you can't, then get out."

The stockholders got angry when Skouras excitedly told them he's about to show them a reel of scenes from various upcoming films. One shouted, "We don't want to see movies, we're here on business." "Wonderful," says Skouras, "roll the film."

Before the meeting we screened what Levathes had sent in from the studio on *Cleopatra*. Ridiculous bits and pieces of scenes, nothing that gives any idea of the picture itself. Skouras said, "Seal up the can and send it back."

Charlie's back—and back to being Charlie again. There is another new company executive committee now which Charlie is on. Charlie says, "We are running things now," meaning I suppose he's back on the team and the pressure has eased a little.

Love,

Jack

Rome, May 19

Dear Jack,

Thanks for sending the letter and the clips. They just came and I hasten to write back so that this can go in the air mail over the weekend, and with luck you'll have it Monday. There are two things I can't describe, my joy at finding mail or cables from you, and my indecision about whether or not I like it here (all in all) or to put the latter another way, how much—to what degree—I hate it. I won't bore you with all that.

The apartment, now that we are newly installed in it, is very okay and a relief from the hotel. It's a penthouse and apparently great when the elevator works, which from first indications is every so often. Magnificent terrace with a view of three-quarters of Rome. It's in the heart of old Rome, just where Golda wanted to be, none of that Parioli convenience for her. A few steps from the Pantheon, from Piazza Navona. The apartment itself has a little of faded elegance about it, the grandeur of a furnished suite at a good hotel worn a little into comfort. We like it. And the Penns are lovely, as you had said, and Golda sees a lot of Sheila by day; I think they will make a thing of going to the beach at Frigene.

As for me, I work. By night I am just dead. The legit American press group here is first-rate, but occasionally one from a different breed crawls out of the woodwork. I mean your friend —— of course. He loathes you, too. Our first meeting went well. We parted (forever I hope), friends. He wants to do a series on the film; I tried to convince him *Cleo* was old hat by now. He brought up *Gente* and the maid's story (which it's assumed hereabouts he ghosted) and I condemned it best, I thought, by saying peephole journalism—what the butler saw, what the maid did, etc.—is okay in London and in Italy, but thank God in the Ewe-nited States we don't stoop to yellow journalism of this repulsive and unprofessional kind, except of course for *Confidential* and the New York *Enquirer*. He muttered that *Confidential* has toned down (probably they wouldn't buy the story from him), and his laugh at the *Enquirer* made me think that that market probably hadn't occurred to him. He did pick me up on the word "butler" and said a respectable magazine like *Cosmopolitan* was going to run the Taylor's butler story, which I didn't know.

There's been an interview with Mansfield knocking Taylor as a bad mother! Which is really a bum rap because she is devoted to her kids. It doesn't break in the States as far as we know, but turns up all over the Italian papers. Sheer nonsense! So when I say "work" is tiring I mean because it's so damned debasing. Maybe all of it was appropriate to the colorful, scandalous and then glamorous best days of Hollywood; and maybe Hollywood made a mistake in switching over to the girl-next-door-just-like-you image, because the public didn't want that, and by the time they found out the girl-next-door was really living, between pictures, in a mental institution in Connecticut, it was too late to retrieve their interest. The world had changed.

Sybil is here to visit Richard. Thursday's ruckus was that Elizabeth couldn't work. She stayed up crying all night and her eyes were too swollen to shoot. That's when we invented the switch to the Moongate set to take advantage of the good weather and thus finish there and return the costly set we've been renting. However, Liz did work, starting in the Mausoleum yesterday, and she volunteered to work today (a Saturday when she didn't have to) to make up for Thursday. This also meant she couldn't go to Paris this weekend as threatened. So this week could be counted as OK.

Our story on the Ischia delay is that we are finishing almost everything here first, to be able to cut costs by returning set space that we are then finished with here. So it's not really a delay, but a transposition of time. See? By the way, I understand there are the necessary services in Ischia for getting the word out, and also there's to be a twice-a-day courier from Cinecittà, so that mail service will be good. It's two or three hours by train from Rome to Naples, and then the water crossing to Ischia. Phones and cables will probably be precarious.

Wanger got the word a day or two ago about Skouras' going into the hospital, prostate, today. He did look bad when he was here. At his age, in his condition, this is bad, isn't it?

Today's story: A delegation of parents, hairdresser, faggots and other members of the court went with Richard to Bulgari's and purchased a bauble Elizabeth had previously suggested to him she wanted. Burton presented it to Taylor the other night, just after Sybil returned, and she was overjoyed to receive it but told him he was too extravagant. It seems to me that considering she has raised his picture price to $500,000 per film, this was the least he could do to show his appreciation. It is reported that she asked him if he didn't think, now that Sybil was here, that he ought to buy something for her, too. He agreed, and they settled on his buying something worth only about one-quarter of what he had spent on Liz. It's all terribly romantic. Next, on the set, Taylor is showing the damn thing off to everybody, but Richard doesn't want it to get into the press because Sybil will find out. He doesn't care about the Italian papers really, just the British. He and Mank asked me to keep it out of the papers, but about a hundred people on the set must know about it already, and about a thousand of Wanger's royal friends must know it too. If this isn't a concrete example of how appalling the work is, I don't know what I can offer you that's better.

One last, to end on a cheerier note: Mank is the ultimate snob on Taylor. Where everybody's trying to be close to her, and Wanger wants to get her to his parties for royalty, Mank turned down her bid to take her out last Tuesday night, when Sybil was here.

That's for now—N.

Dear Jack,

Forgive my not waiting for a response to my letter posted last
Saturday which you probably have this morning—I know we must
keep some semblance of order or we'll never know where we stand.
But I realized yesterday that one major thing (it doesn't even need
a response, so it shouldn't throw out of line what you may be writing me today) was completely overlooked by me.

And that is, the very best part. As you had said it was, seeing the
rushes after work at around six o'clock most nights with Joe, that's
the best of it all. I try to sit behind him and soak up a little of what
he knows and all of what he says.

Outside of the projection room one night last week he had a
comment about how much her diction has improved from the first
part of the film. Had I noticed, comparing these nightly rushes
with the assembled footage we saw a few weeks ago? I certainly
had. He says he told her it's a result of Burton. On the other hand,
he was worried that night when Burton came up with a very Bronx-
like and uncultivated tone in some speech. He told them, he said,
that just because she's beginning to sound like Burton is no reason
for Burton to begin to sound like Eddie Fisher.

Friday night—and this essentially is what I forgot when I wrote
you on Saturday—we saw an hour of the Procession. Taylor looked
awful, very grim, am sure all will say it's a double in the long shots,
and that in close-ups they probably propped her up to sit in the
scene. Couple of great shots, of course, but why didn't Mank try
to make it alive as though it were living history, happening now;
maybe a zoomar lens to give it newsreel immediacy, to move in on
her and then out? Nothing. Well, the hour ended and everybody
told Joe how great it was.

He then did the best 20-minute scene I ever saw. He told them
how it stank, but he really told them. He also gave Wanger the
shivers by saying he wants to do it over—6,000 extras! Just about
everything was wrong, to hear Joe tell it. Everyone did badly, said
Joe, but "I take all the responsibility." Sounding like an Einfeld
meeting, or me after a première, he said quote do I have to do everything around here unquote. Meaning, the horses were wrong,
the crowd or parts of it pushed the wrong way, areas weren't filled

with people, the red carpet is in some shots but missing in others, there are pieces missing to make the movement connectable, Taylor looks stooped over by the weight of the gold costume, the child makes faces because of the lights, and more and more like this, but finally—and this he's right about, it's amazing he can be that objective—the wink Taylor gives Harrison as the culmination of all the panoply is just *awful*. The whole point of the scene, after all the pageantry, is that it is a Mankiewicz spectacle, not the De Mille kind: and the intimate, humanizing, personal, comic-dramatic conclusion is the wink. Well, it falls flat.

One other reference to De Mille. Joe, with his eyes blazing as they can, tells us all (grouped around him on the projection room steps) that he has been saying for seven months you can't shoot the Procession with orders barked in Italian through a loudspeaker to 6,000 people. But nobody listens. You need group leaders in costume, mixed into the crowd, responsible for relatively small units —*you* go here, *you* fill in there—the way De Mille did it. "De Mille knew how to do it, and I have never been able to shoot a big scene like this the way I want to, because nobody will ever listen to me."

They are trying to assure Joe there is enough usable footage with shrewd cutting to bring it off. Also they will do a lot of extra work with small groups of guards, horsemen and others to fill in for what's missing. But Joe insists that they get Taylor again to redo the wink shot (pressure from New York to finish or no pressure) in a studio with a portion of the Sphinx and a portion of a crowd or, if necessary, just against a bluebacking. So I guess it will be done. Fascinating.

One afterpiece—when I told Joe his picture will overcome his fears about *Time*, he said he's sure they will write a review saying Mankiewicz' *Cleopatterer* is "all talk." He also worries needlessly about *The New Yorker*, and I told him it's very different now: Brendan Gill is an intelligent man who likes movies.

All our best,
Nathan

New York, May 21

Dear Nat,

Thanks for all the recent poop, posted just two days ago. I had a marvelous lunch at Sardi's with Bosley Crowther. He seemed to enjoy eating with anyone who was so close to *it*. As a matter of fact, and this is no idle crap, I am treated everywhere with a certain reverence for having been part of *it*. A couple of people stopped by the table at Sardi's, making me feel like a real celebrity, telling Crowther, "You must be important, having lunch with the man everyone wants to talk to." The head is so big I can't fit into the new car!

So we're back and loving everything, tasting everything and enjoying life in New York as we have never loved it before. Strange as it may seem, I'm enjoying the hectic life at 20th. Irwin Allen is here with *Five Weeks in a Balloon*, we have a *Gigot* screening for Jackie Gleason's pals Monday, and *Lisa* and *Caligari* open this week, with a *Hobbs* sneak next week. So you can see what kind of a life it is. Strangely, I'm enjoying it.

Longest Day opens October 4 at the Warner. Charlie seems to seriously believe we have a great film, but I am still scared. I feel the documentary flavor will persist, and no woman I have talked to cares about the film. I hope I'm wrong, but even the trailer footage scared me a little bit.

Forgot to tell you all-importantly that Dorothy is blooming, feels well, and a good deal done for her in Italy was wrong—not injurious, but things like wrong pills for nausea. What they gave her was *not* for nausea. The pills she's been given here have helped 100%. But don't get me wrong, I *hate Italy*. (But you I like.)

Love,
Jack

98

Rome, May 25

Dear Jack,

What a week! No, no, no, you didn't tell me it would be like this. Not like this. I last wrote on Monday. Let me try to recap on what's gone on since, though I may mix in here some of the topics which have been going in the daily business correspondence.

To flash back first to Tuesday. It has been a week of visitors, but Tuesday was *our* day. Our friends Richard and Mimi got in from Moscow and Warsaw on their way back home, and are spending these few days here. Richard is also our broker, you may recall, but the way the market has been going I have suggested perhaps he should have stayed in Moscow and tried Communism, having failed (this week) so utterly at capitalism. I look down at the calendar on my desk and expect to see 1929 the way in movies they always let you see the word *Titanic* as the ship pulls away. So on Tuesday everyone came out to Cinecittà; we had lunch on the lovely commissary terrace, the sun and the trees at their most beautiful, and as though on cue, Taylor and Burton disporting their costumed selves for all to see. The lunch may not be great, but it's a hell of a floor show.

Afterwards we went on to the closed Mausoleum set where work has been going so well as we get closer and closer to the moment when Cleo is to be bitten and die. The feeling of tension grows, because once we have that, obviously nothing—whatever *could* happen—would interfere with our having a complete-able (if that's a word) film; but also because once we have that, isn't Fox going to say "Enough!" and refuse to let Joe finish the many missing and vital scenes that come before the death, which are yet to be shot. In a week or so, if all goes well, that will be *the* dilemma.

On the set, fabulous in its cold, glittering gold feeling of shining stone, torch fires blazing and flickering across Cleopatra's face as she makes ready to die, Mank (who is also a client of Richard's) gave Dick a warm welcome. We were on the set three hours, Mank and Dick talking privately between takes. At one point in their conversation, Elizabeth came over about something and Joe introduced her to Richard, but Dick muffed his intention to say "Hello, I've heard a lot about you."

At one point we were joined in the very tight corner which was

99

the only place visitors could, without interfering, watch the two scenes that were being shot—one a Burton close-up, Taylor off camera; the other of the two of them—by a delegation including Billy Goetz and Irving Lazar. A quick sample of Goetz will do: Doc Merman, working hard, drops whatever he's doing to come up and say hello to Irving, and after he leaves Goetz says to Lazar, "Who is that?" to which Lazar says, "That's Doc Merman. He used to work for you."

And Irving: Ten of us squashed in, watching the forbidden-to-watch scene, trying not to breathe, and he whips out a million-dollar camera which takes a) film b) stills c) probably switches from b/w to color and d) has a silencer on it which permits him, he thinks, to shoot even during the take itself. Only with the silencer it makes more noise than the Todd-AO cameras, but he blithely goes on doing this though Mank, Merman, Taylor's man, Burton's man (let alone me) are aware of it and uncomfortable about it and about the fact that nobody has the guts to stop him. He complained finally that he didn't have enough light, and stopped himself.

Glad to know (we have word here) that Skouras' operation went well and that he is all right. I sent to Leonard Lyons but am reminding you here:

> Spyros Skouras, 20th president, is recuperating from an operation at St. Luke's this week. Before he checked in he did a checkup of his company's big films now in production in Europe: *Cleopatra*, *The Longest Day* and *Nine Hours to Rama*. He said to a visitor the other day, "I spent a very interesting week with Caesar, Eisenhower and Gandhi."

Also there was something I sent—you have a copy, it's either to Dorothy or Earl—about Taylor's "aspixiation" coming up this week. Please check.

Wednesday Carl Foreman came out. He left Liz a script to peruse. But it seems, though this floors me, that she reads only *her* passages, marked in red, never anyone else's. Jack Cominsky, who is the publisher of *Saturday Review*, came at the invitation of Peter Treves. He and his wife seemed extremely pleased by the reception they got, including an hour's visit to the closed set to watch Elizabeth and Roddy making a scene. We agreed that Mankiewicz was ripe for a piece on the literary side of *Cleopatra,* and he was pleasantly surprised by my assurance that Joe would talk to Hollis Alpert if he came over to do such a piece. I wrote you about that separately, of course, but remark on it here because I think this could be very important for restoring the "image" on the film, and Hollis will "see" it as we do, and I know I can prevail on Joe to break the rule and see Hollis. So let me know.

Roddy and Erna were extremely helpful and hospitable with the Cominskys. The *Saturday Review* is her favorite magazine. Have I said enough for Erna's reminiscences? Her saga of Brothers Joe and Herman, from *Skippy* to *Citizen Kane,* is really something. I'm enchanted with that stuff, you know. But for reminiscences, to get on that for a minute, Walter's are the most wonderful: Gloria Swanson, when she was the Taylor of her day, had the same tart tongue and the same imperiousness. One day her leading-man-to-be followed her into Jesse Lasky's office, a nice, deferential guy. When they left, Lasky said, "*He* will never be a star." Better, and recent: When Jerry Wald said they weren't going to use John Stride in *Ulysses* because he wants $50,000, Wanger said, "What's the matter? He didn't ask for enough?" Best, and current: WW showed me Liz's childish scrawl on a scrap of paper. Her terms for *Justine,* which she's after him to let her do. She is asking "$1,000,000 for Elizabeth Taylor and 7% of the gross, and $500,000 for Richard Burton and 7% of the gross. (signed) Elizabeth Taylor." Wouldn't you grab it if you could?

Another visitor, Harold Mirisch [the film producer and one of the Mirisch Brothers]. Afterwards, Joe complaining bitterly that Fred Zinnemann just got an upped deal on *Hawaii* because it's turning out to be a bigger, more difficult project than first imagined. But not Fox, not *Cleopatra.*

Another bulletin: A day's shooting must be done over because the footage was spoiled in transit to the Coast! Difficult stuff, too, involving Burton hitting Taylor and her back-flipping (weak back), all of which Joe had persuaded her to do herself (no double). 25 May

That's been the kind of week we've had. Today we're in trouble. Big row after the show Frank Sinatra gave in Rome last night. ✓ Burton wouldn't take her home; she left and stayed out all night;

didn't sleep, but came in to work today—only she can't do the death scene as we had hoped. So they are doing her stretched out, already dead, and will try to persuade her to work again tomorrow (Saturday) as she did last Saturday. She has worked the Mausoleum faithfully for seven work days in a row, seems to be aware of the besetting panic to finish before the day they stop the money, and is plenty irked by the innuendo given out at the stockholders' meeting that the picture is all but finished when in point of fact it is far from. Anyway, today she is in "no condition," as who is with these 11-hour days? Tomorrow she may make an honest man out of Skouras yet.

Love,

Nat

P.S. Also, had a very nice session with Elizabeth in her trailer yesterday—ah, envious world—at which she approved virtually all the remaining Pete Turner [the photographer] material, and she saw his picture story in—and great cover on—*Show*. The only thing which will disturb Pete is that the three or four pieces of color she didn't approve, I couldn't persuade her to simply let me mark "killed" and return. At that point, Elizabeth took a long pair of scissors off her dressing table and cut them to ribbons, by way of making herself better understood presumably. She has, as you can see, fairly limited powers of expression. This does widen the usual range from "crazy" (favorable) to "balls" (un-). Tell Pete she did giggle over my story of the day he walked out on Greg and me to cover the snow in "Dickens' London" for *Esquire*. He was projecting his slides of her on the wall of his New York apartment, the phone rang, they told him it was snowing in London, he grabbed his passport and coat, and ran for the plane, leaving us looking at Elizabeth Taylor.

■ ■ ■ ■ ■ ■ ■ ■ ■ ■ ■ ■

New York, May 28

Dear Nat,

I have your Friday letter. Also a nice letter from Walter Wanger addressing me as "Dear Dr. Schweitzer" and complimenting me on my missionary work among press people in New York in educating them about the true *Cleopatra*.

Crowther destroyed *Lisa* (you must have the clip by now) and said that the ads for it are misleading. From the moment I read it I knew it meant trouble. Charlie is gray this morning. He has a note from Rosenman saying that the Crowther attack should be discussed at the meeting of the new executive committee today. "See what I have to go through!" he keeps saying to me.

The real madness here—the spirit of let's-shut-down-*Cleopatra*-before-they-shut-us-down—is going back to the feverish high of two weeks ago, if it ever subsided. You, as you may have heard by now, are to be blessed by a delegation of Mosk, Otto Koegel [Fox chief legal counsel] and Levathes later this week. Can't really say if they are acting *for* SPS while he's laid up in the hospital or acting *because* he's laid up. . . . When the whole management turmoil started, it lacked a focus. Boy, it sure got it in *Cleopatra*. Is it to be Skouras' Folly or Skouras' Victory? Funny how you want him to win. Maybe it dates back to all those boardroom sessions, and meetings in his office, and speech-writing days. I don't know. Maybe it's just the affectionate running gag all these years of "Why don't you make babies, Jack?" or—what was it with you?—"Why do you look so worried? Why don't you smile?" We're having a baby, all right, but what do you have to smile about?

Chins up,
Jack

■■■■■■■■■■■■

Dear Jack,

I have a real question for Skouras and Co.: do they know *The Leopard* is being shot in Italian? Charlie was annoyed when I asked him weeks and weeks ago in New York; he said, of course it's being shot in English, they all speak English. Well, it's not, and they don't. Everybody—except Lancaster—will have to be dubbed; he'll speak English, Alain Delon French, and the others Italian. Will it be another case of *The Law*, probably great in the original, but that absurd *Where the Hot Wind Blows* in the dubbing? Does anybody know? Does anybody care? It gets worse from the company which somehow lived through *Snow White and the Three Stooges*, *The Right Approach*, *All Hands on Deck* and *The Fiercest Heart*. I gather from letters from Charlie that we're going to have difficulty on press-and-photographer visits on *The Leopard* and *The Condemned of Altona*. Some question of ethics and propriety in Fox paying some of the cost of these visits. I guess the Old Jedge, now that he's running the new committee, thinks it's "payola." Pretty naïve of the Old Jedge. And now that we have *State Fair*, why don't we also go back to remaking *David Harum* or *Judge Priest*, and for the latter why not star Samuel Rosenman? He can also re-write the script, and that would save a salary. I probably shouldn't digress to this, but *The Leopard* and *Altona* are on my mind, and it does broaden the narrow limits of a self-centered *Cleopatra*.

This morning they were still playing around on the set with the real asp, and the basket of fake figs with the phony asp, and, as it looked like she was going to get it, I wanted to go out there.

Just then Jacopo [Jacopozzi, AP photo chief in Rome] came into my office to look through the contacts. I didn't want him around if we got the call that Liz is doing it. No pictures, please. In New York they want to exploit the end of *Cleopatra*; here they want to keep it quiet so that they can keep going without a) the money being cut off and b) Sybil coming running, as apparently all think she will on the signal that the film is done and Burton doesn't have to go on playing-the-game. But what's the name of the game? (Do you want negs, Jacopo? Do you want prints, Jacopo? Take what you want. Only go, Jacopo!) At that moment we got the call, I slipped away from Jacopo, and hurried to the set. Later I cabled you.

Phil Dunne is here today. Is he going to do *The Agony and the Ecstasy?* What imagination! But of course I refrained from mentioning the reception of *Lisa*.

Will keep in touch,

Nat

■■■■■■■■■■■■

BRODSKY   NEW YORK   MAY 28
WE HAVE IT STOP SHE IS DEAD LOVE WEISS

[*A phone call from Brodsky to Weiss, May 29*]

BRODSKY: Hello, Nat. Got your cable yesterday. Everybody is very excited.

WEISS: Not here. We have big production announcements today, like we're starting over. I'll write you today.

BRODSKY: What do you mean?

WEISS: Like I keep telling you, Jack, there's a lot more to do. The death scene was the most important because it would be tricky to double, and you couldn't finish the picture in some form without it. But that doesn't mean the picture is finished. There's much more to do, and it's important, but they are going overboard.

BRODSKY: I wrote you, you are having visitors later this week.

WEISS: I know, I know.

BRODSKY: They'll stop it.

WEISS: That's no solution either. You go this far, you have the chance of turning out the finest film that's ever been done, and now they are going to compromise it or ruin it?

BRODSKY: Look, it's the worst stock market slump in 33 years, they are panicky; Levathes is asking them to finish the picture today.

WEISS: Look, Jack, Erna says if they tell Joe to finish the picture this week he's going to have news for them. He's going to say, "It's finished now," and walk off. "They may call his bluff," I said. And she said, "I have news for you, he's not bluffing." I think she's right. Let them try to make sense out of it without him and without letting him finish. Christ, if they had let him prepare it properly in the first place, would this be happening?

BRODSKY: There's nothing we can do about it. Though in a way I think we did it.

WEISS: What do you mean?

BRODSKY: I think all the breaks today on the news that the asp did its work has them all hot about closing down the picture right away.

WEISS: Who? Skouras? Levathes?

BRODSKY: Skouras. Levathes. Moskowitz. Michel.

WEISS: Aren't they unbelievable?

BRODSKY: Isn't it all?

WEISS: I have a lot more to tell you. I'll write you.

BRODSKY: Love to all.

WEISS: Goodbye, Jack.

Rome, May 29

Dear Jack,

Just got off the phone with you and don't know what to say first. Only last night we looked at the footage on tests made near Alexandria, scouting locations there, and Joe liked them very much. Remember, first comes Ischia, and we're not even ready to go there yet. This morning—with Elizabeth asped only yesterday—there are new production notes which call for an August 6 start in Egypt! So when you call and say the Big 3—this week's version of the Big 3, but the cast of characters shifts without there being any real change—are coming this week to stop the film at once, I'm confused.

Maybe the August 6 announcement for Egypt and the subsequent conversation and discussion about where this army would be placed and that army would be placed, and how many thousands of this and thousands of that would be needed, refers to another picture: maybe we're going to go right into *Justine* without taking a break. Now that Joe has caught up to the production and finished his night-writing, maybe someone caught him relaxing and figured it was time to get him working again—on *Justine*.

If my tone strikes you as irritable, know that it is authentic. The Cinecittà jungle does have that effect. I've also had a bit too much of the fawning-over of late. I would give a battle or a barge or two to have it over with sooner, but it's ludicrous to know that both art *and* commerce may be jeopardized at this stage, and to be helpless to do anything about it.

Withal, it would be unfair to say the situation is all black. For one thing, you're on the set with Mank, endlessly witty and wise; with WW, as beguiling an aristocrat as he is an historian; Burton, mindful though I am of Scofield, probably the best of his generation; there's watching the dailies and being on the set of the ultimate film, and I was, after all, born a movie bug. Less instructive and stimulating is Miss Taylor, but she is vivacious, vivacious as a child can be. If she is not your own, you find that only of passing interest. And soon, if not already, she will be too old for a child's vivacity.

I got off; I guess I was trying to see the bright side because of the new chilling fear that we are to be stopped short—short of the company having in *Cleopatra* the Godsent chance to recover itself. As Vincent Canby said in *Variety*, *Cleopatra* isn't just a movie, it's a corporate annuity, and as such it's cheap at 30 million dollars.

Today is the last day Taylor will work at the studio here in Rome. Tomorrow we go to Torre Astura. This afternoon was devoted to the retakes for the film that was spoiled in transit. Part of it the slapping stuff. Part of it a Burton solo that is magnificent, and inspired by Elizabeth at his feet (out of camera range). The best of it, in these scenes, parallels Sybil (Rome) and Cleo (Egypt). And in one shot Cleo walks into the scene wearing a gold headdress and you know it's Liz's blond wig that inspired it. Incredible, and so devilishly clever. Audiences will flip. And on the set when Liz must do an Oedipus-scream of discovery—what do you think she screams? She screams, "Sybil!" And goes around crowing, "A *bissel* Sybil." She's Jewish now, you know.

Again, thanks for the phone call, and let me know if anything breaks that I ought to know before the Big 3 arrive later this week.

The very best,
Nat

BRODSKY: Hello, Nat, can you hear me?

WEISS: Not very well. What's up, Jack?

BRODSKY: Just got your letter of Tuesday. Nothing much to say, but won't have time to reply before the delegation gets to Rome tomorrow, so I thought I'd call.

WEISS: Thanks. Are they on schedule?

BRODSKY: I think they are ahead of it. They were due on the weekend, but I think they will be there tomorrow.

WEISS: We'll be working at Torre Astura tomorrow. Today's a religious holiday here, there's no work on the set, but we will be working in the office of course.

BRODSKY: I don't think they'll go down to Anzio to the set. They'll probably meet with Mank and Walter or Merman or Rogell or whoever at night and on the weekend at the hotel.

WEISS: That's what we figure. You know, if they set a reasonable deadline a month or two away, I think Joe could manage. Fox must be able to say it's finito in six weeks or eight weeks, but not sixteen or eighteen. That's crazy, but so is trying to stop us dead right now. We need Ischia. We need Egypt.

BRODSKY: They're talking about moving it back to Hollywood. Stopping now in Rome, seeing what they have, and then finishing up what needs to be done in Hollywood.

WEISS: That will look crazy.

BRODSKY: I know, I know. But Skouras looks worried. The Wall Street group is in control. It looks as though Levathes is their boy. They know what he tells them. At least they've got Michel out. I don't know, I don't know.

WEISS: I'm beginning to think we know more than they do. They don't really know we exist, but the fact is I think we know more about the company and films and what to do about it than they do. In what other company in a state like this would two flunkies be this close to the core of it so that they *see* it better than the guys running it?

BRODSKY: It doesn't help . . . and it's a terrible connection; I can't even hear it all.

WEISS: Let my last word be on Skouras and Einfeld. At least presidents and vice-presidents with open doors are better than companies where you never really get to meet the president.

BRODSKY: A lot of good it does us. Before you hang up, remember, write me or call me or something as soon as you know anything.

WEISS: One other thing, Jack. I think Mank is really sore at us for publicizing the significance of the asp scene.

BRODSKY: That's silly. You couldn't keep that quiet. They ask every minute, there are spies all around.

WEISS: I know, Jack, but he gripes anyway—and he says it makes Elizabeth look like some kind of nut who had to be carried through it, which she's not. After all, he still has a lot of work to do with her.

BRODSKY: Okay. Anything else?

WEISS: No, that's it. I'll write. Goodbye, Jack.

Dear Jack,

I am looking forward to our visitors today. I'll go to the airport to meet them, but wonder if any information will trickle out to us over the weekend. My happiness over the fact the various "finishing" stories are breaking well back home is in conflict with the new production schedule—which has us doing location work for Pharsalia, then to Torre Astura, then to Ischia, then a return to Cinecittà to finish on one of the stages that must be relinquished by July 2, then back to Ischia to finish with Taylor by July 7, then back to Torre Astura to finish by August 4, then to Egypt to finish finish by the end of August. I swear they look hungrily at Egypt like a fresh start; maybe I wasn't too far off, maybe it is only a dry run for *Justine*. *Flash from Charlie*—I didn't say I'd heard from you yesterday—with the tip that when the Big 3 arrive today they are giving Mank notice that the picture must end by July 31. Then he cut off abruptly, saying he couldn't talk any more. Are there gunmen stalking the halls of Fox now?

That would be an intelligent and reasonable compromise, I think. It would avoid making a disaster of *Cleopatra* which would only boomerang at Fox anyway. Yet I've felt that the madness of one in-group after another trying to wrest control of Fox this past year, and apparently not one knowing what to do with it if they did succeed, had reached such a dizzy peak that *Cleopatra*, the one thing that might save them, would be endangered. You know, it could have been anything that would have become the focus of the sickness at 20th; *Cleopatra*, like a willing girl, just happened to be available.

I really must go off to pick up our guests. Wanger and Rogell have been preparing the "summit." It's like a mystery story. You tell something to one person, a few minutes later you are called by someone else who gives you another version of the story you told to someone else just a few minutes before. One office is already refiguring the production schedule to July 31 instead of August 31, even though the offer hasn't been made yet, and up to a few hours ago we thought maybe we'd be shut down tomorrow. By this calculation, maybe Egypt would be eliminated for now, and after Ischia the film would go back to Hollywood for editing—and later on, if necessary, they would organize themselves again to make the little jaunt from Hollywood to Egypt for additional filming.

The word is that Joe the Mosk will talk turkey to Joe the Mank, and that Otto K. is along as a witness in our Kafkan Trial.

Oh, yes, to add to the farcical tone, Wanger cabled them to hold off until Monday, but by this time they were in Paris and now are en route here. Gotta go now.

Love,
Nat

■■■■■■■■■■■■

New York, June 2

Dear Nat,

I know the meetings are on, and I have nothing more to say than I said on the phone and in my cables, but I've got to get this off, said succinctly, for what it's worth—and maybe you can get it over to someone:

I feel, as you know, that Mank should be left alone to make his movie, and that anything they do to tamper with it now will make it less of the movie we know it can be. The way they are going, they'll make it a dull movie. Maybe Joe was wrong to think he could do it all himself, but that harm is done and they're cutting off their noses to spite their faces.

As before,
Jack

■■■■■■■■■■■■

Dear Jack,

It has been rough. Except for the one business letter written
you two days ago, I've not written at all. Therefore this letter spans
from last weekend (the arrival of the Big 3) to now. I leave to your
phone call last night and mine to you this morning, when I woke
you up at home—for which I apologize but remind you that you
once called me at three in the morning when we were here at the
Grand and you were in New York last September—the "unofficial"
matters of business we discussed. I make only this comment: the
idiocy of our having to handle legitimate press activities in this
manner, fearful of charges of payola, is something even the Italians, devious though they are, can't understand. Their dealings
with other American film companies in the past hadn't prepared
them for this nonsense. All this might as well be Greek, which in a
basic sense, of course, it is.

Now then, to try to pick up the pieces. I am tired; I had just "settled down" to Rome when it seems to me all hell broke loose. Oh,
yes, let me say, when money is laid out or tickets bought from here
for anybody, don't think that Wanger's permission means anything. It will still eventually come back to Charlie. To draw a parallel, just as in matters of booking the picture, Mank nor anyone
else will mean anything. It will still come back to Fox in New
York. I see that they were stopped by Zanuck from destroying
Longest Day by booking it everywhere the day the print is dry, but
Cleopatra they may be free to fuck up.

Now, to go back to last weekend. The reason Wanger tried to
head the Big 3 off before they got here is that Mank was going to
Ischia for the weekend to scout the setup there. He saw them only
Friday and Sunday nights. They were adamant: Taylor was washed
up this week, and must finish by the end of it; the picture could go
to June 30 but no longer, and he could do what he wanted within
that time; and Wanger was "out" as of that moment. Monday
morning the picture was screened for them. They were on the commissary terrace for lunch, Mosk and Pete even stopped by to shake
hands and say hello to me, but not too long after that Pete cracked
to Wanger that there was no longer any need for a publicity unit
here and they could start saving that money now.

Wanger and Merman lunched with the Big 3 that day and looked grim. After rushes—which ran late both nights—on Monday and Tuesday, they had more meetings with Mank. We didn't quit the projection room until eight on Monday night, and after that on Tuesday, no time of night to start to do battle.

Wanger looked so old and crushed on Monday, the day they told him not to even come in any more. But soon afterwards he told me he has his lawyers working on it, and not to worry, he's been through these things before.

Yesterday, Wednesday, down at Torre Astura location (we had a press junket, of which more below), and Joe told me that he walked out on the final meeting Tuesday night. Wanger told me he tried to defend Joe, but Pete shouted that Mank had not known what he was doing or how to make a picture, causing WW to say to him, "Pete, don't let your failure go to your head."

The Big 3 departed yesterday, and by today WW looks better. This morning I had the call from New York which said that the new "finish date" was July 17 for the picture, June 19 for Taylor. The first was new to him, the second the edict-carriers had arrived at on a compromise, even though they said they were neither able to deal nor to negotiate (is there a difference?). They even pulled out a letter from SPS telling Mank he could not interfere, in case Mank was thinking of turning to him for help (which he was). This morning's report is encouraging, but not of course binding. Mank is also heartened by a letter—Walter showed it to me—from Rex Harrison to WW saying he would finance 20th doing the missing Pharsalia battle sequence needed to open the picture intelligibly, because he feels it is essential to the film, and after seeing the agony Mank is experiencing he would like to make a contribution! I never saw a letter that touched me more. P.S. I've never even met the man.

Joe is so defeated and yet he keeps working and pushing on—he didn't pack his bags and walk or run out. Joe tells me he argued with the combine that they will have "the first indoor movie in Todd-AO" if they didn't let him finish what had to be done, but they said it didn't matter, there was just no more money. He says he's finished June 30 unless he hears to the contrary. If press people to whom he would talk do show up, I warn you he is going to *talk*—as only he can. Of course that will end it for him on *Justine*, which could be the greatest of them all, but he says that is over. The work he did belongs to Fox, more than that he will not do, there can be no inducement to work for Fox as it is presently constituted, again. In any event, the Big 3 overshot their mark; if there was to be an ultimatum, it couldn't be June 30, it had to be at the earliest July 31. I know there is a large quota of plays about such power-plays in the literature, as we of the library say, but don't you think there's a good one in this situation?

Yesterday's press outing was something, considering the tensions in the air as a result of all the foregoing. And yet *Cleopatra* goes on, facing her audience bravely and with a smile. We had busloads come down to our Alexandrian shores with the water lapping at the edge of the stone steps, and our Egypt glistening in the sun. It was a perfect day to show off what must be the most impressive setting ever built for the screen.

Before the box lunch we were supposed to do an interesting but harmless scene between Taylor and Hume Cronyn. However, rain had delayed a scene between Taylor and Burton which was scheduled the day before, and suddenly they changed over and decided to do that scene instead. So it was that the press (I'll send you separately a business letter with the list of who was there for the press follow-up) had an opportunity to see Taylor and Burton playfully dueling with one of their children, and then rolling in the grass. Of course there were press photogs as well as reporters, as I suppose you know by now from the wire service pictures that went out last night. It was, shall we say, a scene we had preferred they not see.

After lunch there was a short but eloquent scene in which Antony divorces his wife after the fashion of the time—by proclaiming it three times to the multitudes. Partly because the writing is so overnight-contemporary, to coin a new period, there were regrettable connotations from the point of view of stirring up the press —regrettable that is from the puritan Fox viewpoint, but not damaging I suspect to the box office. It is, in just about every sense, a most peculiarly ambivalent production. As a final topper, for goodwill, don't you think that Burton, who was fluffing his "divorce" speech to the winds repeatedly, didn't suddenly turn to the press group and scream, "Get these people out of here," which left our visitors with exactly the impression they have had all along, which is not the one we should like them to have. Maybe these are the vagaries of press junkets in general, but it has a curiously *Cleopatra* ring.

I am heartened by the rumor that floundering Fox may find its new cleanup wizard in Max Youngstein. It's sure that Fox cannot go on taking in so little a week and needing a million to break even. Doesn't anybody realize that neither the low-quality pix they keep grinding out (*Five Weeks in a Balloon, Lion of Sparta* or *It Happened in Athens*) nor the one-release-a-month of slightly better vintage can bring in what's needed? Yet they haven't succeeded in bringing down the overhead, cost of distribution or cost of studio operation. Of course it can't go on much longer. But, for us, isn't that a reason to play it to the bitter end, to see what three people will finally be left on earth after the bomb finally disintegrates the whole thing?

On the production side, I really didn't believe until you told me that Levathes and Rosenman are going ahead on Goldstein-Moskowitz-type pix like *Take Her, She's Mine* and *Evil Come, Evil Go*. That's a crusher.

All clear? Yes, I thought it was. Or, check one: not at all.

Love,

Nathan

P.S. The real point about being here, I am reminded again, is what I observed tonight when I saw the rushes of the retakes on Burton's magnificent speech. The film ran on a fraction past the scene, and you saw Liz dressed in street clothes rushing into the shot of Antony to deliver a kiss; he looked so startled, it was one of those moments the whole world should see. And this is what *Cleo* is all about. We saw the rushes of the asp death scene, which is subtle, original, and beautiful. The picture is marvelous—or will be if they don't fuck it up. And you forget during the day, and you remember each night when you see the rushes. I must rush if this is to get mailed. N.

■■■■■■■■■■■■

New York, June 11

Dear Nat,

It's a different rumor every day. The news of the morning of course is hard fact: Wanger has been fired. You probably know it there today, or will by tomorrow morning. Fox has cut his salary off. But I think all the sympathy of the press can be thrown to Walter, and anyway, as somebody said to me, "How could they fire him? I thought he owns part of the picture."

I know we have talked of "breaking out" before. You had said that as far as you were concerned, this time away was the logical break with Fox, and Golda insisted it be made a permanent one. Admittedly we had a pact before to try to hold things together— certainly this excellent department will fall apart if we are not here —but with you about to head off to Ischia for one of the many last laps on this picture, the end begins to come into sight. Now, what of obligations?

I for one feel free upon completion of *Cleopatra*. We will have served her, and *The Longest Day*, and all the garbage of years past, extremely well. I've served my time. The rumor factory has not yet produced one hard answer. You know I always speak truth. I believe you are a coward: only a jellyfish could still dream of a knight on a white charger coming to take over and save the Fox damsel. You should never face Golda again if you think you can possibly stay at 20th for any time when you come back.

Get out, get out! Stop thinking of the past, and think of the future. We both have to dynamite our way out of here.

I guess I know now why after missing The Boat a couple of times I had no heart to phone him again. All he keeps saying is, "It'll get better." How? By Levathes becoming president? Rosenman says, "*Lisa* is such a good picture, why didn't it do business?" Spoke to Jerry Wald today and he's as much in the dark as anyone. Don't tell me you honestly believe anything will save this company in our lifetime. The simple fact is that if it should change in five years, by that time we can have advanced beyond anything

119

we could've gotten here . . . so stop deluding yourself that there is a chance here.

Will send you clips on Wanger firing and details as they arrive.

Love,
Jack

■■■■■■■■■■■■

Dear Jack,

Your letter of Monday just came. Just in time, as within the hour we'll be pushing off for Ischia. So let me recount first what's of top import.

Yesterday was the day of the Wanger crisis and he handled himself superbly—as you would have expected him to. I told him he's the noblest Roman of them all. The Big 3 had left here (just one week ago today) agreeing Wanger was still boss (Rogell confirms to me that Koegel used those words); they had left him an edict to see to it that all the finishing dates were accomplished—Taylor June 19, Italy July 4 first unit, six more days allowed first unit in Egypt, second unit winding up July 12 in Italy, etc. All in all it seemed to him and Rogell that they grudgingly realized that he was the boss; but as soon as they left cables started coming from them to Doc Merman (instead of to Wanger, as they would have before on routine business matters), and so he began to realize he was not the boss after all. Now of course there is the story of his being fired leaked to Earl Wilson.

I have a terribly amusing letter from Bosley about the situation here. There may be another Metro story for him in the Fox situation.

We heard that the Monroe-Martin picture is now canceled, so that's another (what?) $1,500,000 write-off loss for Fox. Will it ever end? You are right of course when you say run, do not walk, to the nearest exit.

The fact is they have "fired" Wanger, but apparently the picture is to be allowed to go on and get completed. That's something, anyway. It is something of a relief to know that this at least is not going to be scrapped just when it is within "minutes" of being the finest thing ever. With all the trials here—and I have a feeling Ischia will be worse, judging by the advance tips on the phone, and the exposed-to-the-press conditions there—when we go into the projection room each night for the rushes there is a constant reminder that the picture is what's important, it's all there on the screen, it is *that* good really, and somehow everything seems bearable after that. I repeat myself, but that's it.

Love,

Nat

Dear Nat,

I am glad, and relieved, that you did not burn at my "coward" attack in my previous letter. The frankness between us is understood, and no matter what you ever said to me in a letter, or in person, it would never interfere with my feeling for you. I presume the vice is versa. Not to be faggy, but we are like an old married couple. We may argue, even violently at a point, but we are fated to stick together because what brought us together in the first place is so strong. Right? Right.

The one other topic I want ready for you when this greets you in Ischia is a summary of the spate of rumors of the day. DFZ has been here for a week or so, as you know, and huddling with Rosenman and other biggies on the Fox board. It seems that Zanuck got a flood of letters in Paris from stockholders demanding his return to power. Could it be that they are approaching him about trying to point the nose of this sinking submarine upwards again? (After all, it would be one way for Zanuck to protect *The Longest Day* from being shadowed by the dazzling rays of *Cleopatra*.) Oddly enough, at the same time that DFZ is being wooed to get back into active management of the company in some way, there is a well-founded report around that Zanuck took a beating from Rosenman on the subject of costs being racked up by *Day* for Fox to absorb. To give you a further idea of how topsy-turvy all this is, they have —according to yet another theory—even asked Zanuck to take over *Cleopatra* now that Wanger is "fired," but I think that one must be way out. . . .

Please write first opportunity what it's like at Ischia. And how our "fired" producer is carrying on, as I am sure he must be, producing.

Yours,
Jack

■■■■■■■■■■■■

Ischia, June 18

Dear Jack,

Well, here's a first try at a report from Ischia. It has been impossible to write before this, so this is the first letter of any kind to you since last Wednesday, when I wrote in haste from Evacuation City. Cinecittà always had a temporary air about it, like a wartime housing project outside Washington. Ischia is more like a rest camp.

We got here by *Rapido* to Naples, and then by hydrofoil boat across the Bay. The view of Naples from that circular harbor is as good as I remember it from ten years ago, unmistakably Naples even if under the heat of the sun at the dock everybody looked pretty much as though they were waiting for the special to Fire Island Pines.

Arriving at Ischia was really something, with press covering every arrival, from motorboat to steamer, waiting for Taylor-Burton. Nella's assistant, Nanni, has turned out to be a Faulknerian, an Italian baron, and behind that moody little frame a witty intellectual and an author. How do I know, you may well ask, when at Cinecittà he spoke only Italian and seemed to fail to understand even "Good morning" in English? Because in Ischia Nanni speaks English! I think that's significant, because already in these first days of a long weekend here, one can tell that the atmosphere is less tense, more relaxed than Rome—for everybody. But I am getting ahead of my story.

Nanni has a car waiting for us, and we proceed up and down the hills on the coastline of Ischia—about a 20-minute ride (in very threadbare cabs) from the port to the hotel. As we are approaching the island's heliport, about five minutes from the hotel to which we are heading, there is the deafening sound of a helicopter just above us coming down for a landing. In it of course are Elizabeth Taylor and Richard Burton—making a dramatic arrival which, if they intended it to be a "quiet slipping into Ischia," failed to work because the *paparazzi* were springing out of every bush, zooming past us on motorcycles, and generally creating pandemonium. I suppose our stars will blame us for the resultant press coverage, which I already see in the first clip from the *World-Telly* which arrived today; but 1) they never asked our advice, or told us

123

how they planned to get to Ischia; and 2) they are asking for it when they decide on this grandly absurd entrance.

We were deposited at the Reginella, a mock-Spanish hotel across the street from and seemingly an elegant servants' quarters for the de luxe Regina Isabella hotel, a kind of super-Grossinger's which fronts on the water. Nella had made an earlier trip to Ischia to line up quarters for us and inspect the press security Taylor and Burton would enjoy. Liz and Richard enjoy quite lavish suites on the same floor at the Regina Isabella. Wanger is also there, and Mank is next door to it at a more informal adjunct called The Sporting. Nanni, who is utterly adorable here, uninhibited in his use of English and given to an instant, wry, cynical humor, had looked into the Taylor-Burton quarters earlier in the day (as he had preceded us to Ischia by a day or two); he reports that Liz has a palatial five-room suite to herself, and Burton a comfortable apartment. Was the apartment equipped for Sybil if she should join him, I asked Nanni, and he replied, "It has an icebox." It sounds better in translation.

That complex of Regina Isabella, Reginella and Le Sporting is owned by Rizzoli, the Italian Hearst. Surprise, surprise! Who turns out to have the rooms near the stars? *Paparazzi!* They are all over the place, disguised as guests, disguised as employees. You've got to hand it to the Italians. (You might as well; they'll take it anyway.) The first work day Liz went out to work the *paparazzi* attacked; she went flew-ey and couldn't work. We did come up with a natural cover when an explosion incident on one of the barges anchored just off our locations occurred.

One day Wanger asked one of the Italian stringers working for one of the wire services *not* to take a certain picture of Taylor and Burton, and the guy didn't. I later walked into a scene in the hotel where one of the Italians on our picture was giving the photographer hell for *not* taking the shot! She switched her tactics when she saw I was onto her game and sourly told the guy, "We'll give you a prize for not taking that picture!" This at least was in English, but generally it's in Italian and I must say they have us by the balls. But I'm picking up enough to know it ain't kosher. It is, as the man said, a human experience, very instructive, working abroad. This is their game, and I suppose it's silly to try to play it other than by their rules. They really don't think of themselves as "the enemy"; to them this is simply the way business is done. It's just crazy for an American company to try to operate here the way it does at home; you really must play it their way.

We lasted all of one day at the Reginella. Too far from the office which was set up at the Jolly Hotel, and too costly. The Jolly is midway between the Regina Isabella hotel complex described above and most of the sets and the barges where the picture is being shot. It is close to the harbor, where we arrived. If the Regina Isabella is the Carlyle, the Jolly is the local Statler. The production office at the Jolly must ordinarily be the hotel's ballroom and banquet hall but is now the *Cleopatra* HQ. My office therefore is accessible to the hotel terrace on one side, the bar on another, and the swimming pool on a third. It sounds wonderful but it is a little peculiar; also hot, and fairly uncomfortable.

We've been all around the island, very Spanish the island, and it's very picturesque. Good fish; quaint eating; all very much like T. Williams' location for *The Night of the Iguana*. The iguana, by the way, is tasty. But this isn't civilization as far as working conditions are concerned.

The sets at which we have been working the first couple of days are at sea; just the way our board of directors thinks the whole production is. I mean, literally; we do have other sets, on land, but we haven't worked them yet. One is Cleopatra's barge, one is Antony's; we have, you see, *His* and *Hers* barges. To get to hers, I cross (have crossed by myself a few times) yards and yards of planks drifting across open sea (exactly like those obstacle courses I balked at in army training, and ended up at the psychiatrist's for), jump across patches of open sea, scale tilting boards, precariously climb rope ladders. To get to Antony's, a local fisherman is employed to half row, half motor you out, way way out to where the barge is anchored. You may recall that I can't swim. It's a very little, very wet, very unsafe boat. But I go, on one occasion with Herb Mitgang [of *The New York Times*] in tow (he's come to interview Mankiewicz). We arrive at a strategic moment in the filming, I guess, and probably interrupt it. All I recall is Joe Mankiewicz coming down a steep flight of gold stairs (I thought I had drowned and gone to heaven) to assist our arrival and lead us up to the deck of the barge. I tell you, after Ischia, I have lived.

The Penns and Golda discovered (and I spent yesterday afternoon there with them and Herb Mitgang) the best little beach on Ischia, an enchanting cove called Montana. Today work knocked off early, and Herb and I had a date with Joe on the veranda of the Regina Isabella for an interview at cocktail time. More of that in a minute. But when I got back to our hotel Golda thought she had a big coup to tell me: it seems that she and the Penns had returned to Our Cove that afternoon when who turns up for the afternoon—nice terrace restaurant, small private beach, you pay about a dollar to go on it—but Burton and Taylor. Oddly enough, I knew they had been there, because Liz and Richard came through the veranda terrace of the Isabella on their way back from the beach just as Mitgang was doing The Big Interview with Joe. And Herb, who had quietly noted to me that he had not met Liz when he had been on the set watching the filming that morning—I had not been there to introduce him then—and had said the usual thing we all say about who wants to meet actors, it's the directors, producers and writers who interest *him*, nearly fell over when Elizabeth suddenly came up to Joe, him and me. I introduced him to her, and then she took Herb aside and stepped away from us for a few minutes of private talk. This from the girl who won't see any press!

When they rejoined Joe, Richard and me, Herb gave her his account—which he had told us earlier—of how he was taking a photograph of a local native woman of Ischia passing the Regina Isabella with a basket of fruit on her head, when suddenly Miss Taylor emerged from the hotel and inadvertently stepped into his picture. To which Elizabeth said, "You mean like another basket of fruit." Anyway, Taylor-Burton told us they had found *the* best beach on the whole damn island, and it pleasured me to be able to say I had spent Sunday (the day before) on it, and Mank sulkily said he'd heard it was the best but hadn't had time to go. . . .

In the interview, which ran an hour and three quarters, Mank sent out many terribly interesting "waves." Mitgang provoked some of them cleverly. He asked Mank why he had not written about anything more elevated than actors' egos, and didn't he think screenplay writing at best wasn't as good as "real writing"? To which Mank responded that he wants to spend his next years doing both more reading and more writing, and the latter may very well take other forms—plays or novels—and that directing (films, plays) is only an extension of writing for him, like the French "theater film." Mank seemed to feel Mitgang was demanding that he write with a "message," but that at most he wanted his work to make "comments" because he writes out of an interest in people, in behavior, and not out of any slavish devotion to a cause. The session made up for a lot, retracing as it did Joe's whole career, and I wished I could take everything down, but we couldn't very well both be filling notebooks, could we?

I think Mank and Mitgang got on *well*, but not great. Mank didn't help by telling Herb he's suspicious of soft-spoken, sad-eyed writers. All he needed to add was "and of experts on Sicily." He told him so with humor, still he said it. I am not sure Herb accepted without a trace of rancor some vivid, psychiatrically oriented comments, witty ones, he was getting from Mank, and some were shafts that revealed Mank's own weaknesses, but both sides seemed to reach out for and then recoil from any kind of "personal" accusation. Mank dwelt at length on his theory of Liz as a Cinderella for whom the Prince will always turn out to be (figuratively) impotent, and backed it up with a profound study of Liz's having known no life other than the "fantasy" she has acted out since she was a child—the fantasy of life as seen in a Hollywood script. What other life had she ever been exposed to?

The interview also got so rough on Fox I winced, and Mank asked me if he had gone too far. Example: "If they had let me get it ready properly, it would have made a better picture, but it would have cost fifteen million dollars less." As he said, the word "but" must be quoted accurately.

Next morning, June 19

I had to stop there last night; it's early A.M. Let me pick this up and get it out in the very earliest mail which, they tell me, will be the same as if it were mailed last night. I've been up from six to eight this A.M. getting Mitgang and then Bert Stern off this island. Ischia is a very colorful place at six in the morning. Our taxi—a 1929 model—broke down on the way to the helicopter. (If I may telescope a third of a century of progress, apologies to Chicago, in one sentence.) We panicked there for a moment, but another taxi rescued us. I did hear Herb mutter, "Brodsky was right."

To come now to Bert Stern, he quickly saw that his story wasn't

on the "set" but beside it. Only the offstage romantic story is commercial, in his opinion, the angle being that it's not what the world
thinks, it's full of "affection" between them and the latter-day
parallel of a classic romance. He agreed to shoot it, put it away and
sell only with my knowledge, approval and agreement at a given
date closer to the time of release. The saving grace of such a layout to be that Mank would select from the film text quotes that
parallel the pictures, thus linking the affair to the film. It may not
be what the irate stockholders—the puritan ones who write in and
will be, I suppose, among the first to buy tickets—have in mind,
but the commercial results should assuage any guilt feelings attend-
ant to indulging in a little voyeurism.

Also in all of Bert's pictures, Liz is in her Cleopatra eye makeup,
bits of the set are in the background, as Bert shot from Liz's yacht
tied up next to the barge which is the "set" she keeps going onto
and off. Her costume is thrown over her bikini for the film shots.
A real serious Method actress, you see.

One fear is that her sunburn, which gets deeper every day, isn't
going to match the previously filmed interior shots that go with
these barge-top scenes. Another fear: for all the whistle-alarm sys-
tems, sightseers in all kinds of craft come into the camera range
when a shot is being made, driving everybody crazy. Everybody
but Liz, that is; she does her scene, scampers down the rope lad-
der, drops her heavy costume, and rejoins Richard and Bert Stern
and whoever else comes by on the little yacht for sunbathing. She
even got playful on board for one scene. After flubbing a take on
her barge where she's plotting battle strategy on her topo board
(pushing around miniatures to determine, in chess game style, what
the battle moves might be), she screamed out, "Antony, Antony,
you *schmuck*, can't you see you're walking into a trap?" in her best
Yiddish accent.

Bert isn't certain he will get all he needs out of this visit, but he
had to cut it short today because he got the call from Marilyn
Monroe that she will pose for him, and he wants to be on the
Coast tomorrow or Thursday at the latest. This romance story
could be classic: idyllic shots, black-and-white and color, and words
set in big type, the words of romance being quoted from the Mankiewicz script with big big quote marks. Does sound grand. Could

be a memorable, historic photo essay which I've pegged "Last Summer at Ischia."

Sunday one of those things happened that can only happen here. Rizzoli invited Taylor and Burton and various other celebrity guests aboard his huge, glorious, ocean liner-type yacht which is always at the dock in Ischia. They eventually went to Capri for the day and Elizabeth discovered Gracie Fields' Canzone del Mer (which as I recall was "out" by the time we got there ten years ago, but no matter) and, from all accounts, thought it heavenly. I cabled you the list of all sorts of celebrities along—the Terence Rattigan group—as I thought you could use it for columns. At any rate as lunch is being served on the yacht Elizabeth insists that pictures are being taken (it is her usual obsession, of course). Burton tells her she's becoming paranoid. But she says she detects a whirring sound. They throw back the curtains separating the galley from where lunch is being consumed and sure enough there are newsreel *and* still cameras trained on Liz and Richard!

The upshot is that Taylor snubbed Rizzoli in the hotel that night—as well she might. The next day one of the Italians on the picture actually asked Wanger to get a letter of apology from Taylor! Not, mind you, the other way around as it ought to be. I know that they weren't doing anything damaging. Certainly Bert Stern photographing them swimming, sunbathing and kissing is more to the point; but that was done with consent. And the idea of hidden cameras is really too much.

I've been so caught up in the filming and the events here I've not even been able to think of what's happening back home. As of this morning WW says they are still saying "no money after July 1," but we're proceeding on the theory we have until July 8 —that being the latest of the ever-shifting deadlines; however that means end Ischia July 1, do a needed week in Rome, then call it quits. It is said around, however, that Elizabeth and Richard are having so good and relaxed a time here (after the first couple of days even the *paparazzi* eased up, or seemed to, and except for the Sunday-in-Capri incident it's been fairly serene) that they want to stay on until July 8 in Ischia. WW comes up with a switch that's delicious: he says he and Liz, as the heads of the companies that are partners with 20th in this venture, may take it over and throw out Fox! You might say, to give you an item, that instead of Fox releasing *Cleopatra* it will be *Cleopatra* releasing Fox.

I'm written out. Let me hear from you.

Love from Golda too,
Nathan

■■■■■■■■■■■■

New York, June 21

Dear Nat,

Before anything, thanks for the bundle from Ischia.

Before anything else, I have just come down from a screening of
The 300 Spartans. Bob Goldstein was right when he said—in puffing up long ago how wonderful this picture would be—that "we
don't deserve a picture like this." He's right; we don't.

The big piece of news is that there's to be a board meeting on
the 27th which Mike Connolly (in print) and Larry Lipskin (at
Sardi's) [both *Hollywood Reporter* columnists] say will be hot. I
haven't been able to pin down what exactly, but there seems to be
a feeling that something may happen, like closing the studio or
something. We have said so many times that the decisive moment
was at hand only to have it wash out. So let's wait and see. But the
waiting has never been more unbearable.

Charlie is very depressed because, as he puts it, "The IBM ma-
chines sit there and try to run the company." The facts are that
the Judge and friends are at the studio doing the usual reconnais-
sance. SPS is recuperating at home and reportedly doesn't have the
old fight-back left in him. The real deadlock has occurred because,
despite what the papers are saying, there are not just two sides but
three. Two of them have candidates, but the oldest board members are simply waiting for a good enough figure to compromise on.

The trouble now is that there is so little money coming in and
so little on the horizon, that they will have to slash costs and I
fear they may really do some harm. They are busy making all those
old surveys again, but now that there is little revenue coming in,
they may *have* to do it.

The tough thing at the studio is that the board is now afraid to
OK a picture into production. I really can't see *Ulysses* getting an
OK. Charlie is trying to cut wherever he can.

One thing that all this inner turmoil accomplishes for you is that,
for the moment, nobody has given a goddam about the Taylor-
Burton publicity from Ischia. The helicopter arrival got covered
—but nothing scandalous. I must say that both the business of
their kissing (if for Stern I guess this must have been long-lensed
at the same time by the *paparazzi*) and the Capri "adventure"
got covered in the local press, *but* maybe around here nobody has

131

given it a thought because the focus of the company's woes and grief is shifting for the moment from *Cleopatra* to next Wednesday's meeting. Or maybe, with SPS home sick, there's nobody to open the mail in the morning—and so the irate stockholders haven't been heard from yet. I always said whoever goes downstairs to open the mail in the morning will be the boss—and it looks mighty like we don't have one at the moment.

Let me hear. I will let you know.

Marion's mother says it doesn't matter what Richard Burton is doing; but is he Jewish? But Carol cares more about what he's doing. [Marion Zinn and Carol Young were Weiss's secretaries in New York.]

Love,
Jack

Dear Jack,

You will have this a day or two before the meeting on the 27th. Please cable or phone as best you can as we will all be waiting to hear. Wanger doesn't hear from anybody; Rogell and/or Merman may hear from Levathes if anything world-shaking happens, but then I'm not sure Levathes hears from anybody. Is it still a Jim Aubrey-and-Max Youngstein world, crazy as it can be? Or who's on first?

I guess I owe Nella an apology. We were prepared for the wave of Neapolitan press—"the worst kind," she kept saying—from the time we got here. But, after the first flurry of Ischian arrival stuff, I didn't see any press wave descending on us. Admittedly the one day we had the press out on the barge (very difficult under working conditions there), there were some funny things going on, as we couldn't seem to control the official wire-service photogs who wouldn't pay attention to the scene being played which they were free to photograph, but kept sneaking in side shots of the stars at play between takes on their little yacht tied up to the big barge. But I never saw when the *paparazzi* had an opportunity to take those Taylor-Burton kissing shots with a long lens over Bert Stern's shoulder, so to speak. Nella kept saying, behind her Egyptian hairdo and impenetrable sunglasses, a true goddess of inscrutability, "They are all around us," in her mysterious way—pointing to the hills. I guess she was right. Because they were.

Today should be the last day Elizabeth Taylor works on *Cleopatra*—at least the last day she will work on the scenes being shot here in Ischia. But before I get into that, let me recap on an incident of last evening.

We were with the Hollis Alperts last night (they've just come for Hollis to do his piece on the film for the *Saturday Review*) at dinner on the terrace of the Regina Isabella (if I haven't conveyed to you by now just how elegant it is, know that Charles Boyer is staying there now and we had a pleasant few minutes with him and Walter yesterday, but I digress). Afterwards we were joined for drinks on the veranda by an old schoolmate of Hollis' and mine at the New School, one Stella Adler. *She* had just dined at the local pizzeria next door with Elizabeth and Richard—"I'll say that for them, they know how to eat," she remarked. Stella recounted, by starlight of course, how her whole life opened up to her because of The Affair. One day she bought, in addition to her faithful daily purchase of *The New York Times*, a copy of the New York *Mirror* —in order to follow the adventures of Elizabeth and Richard. The things that go on, she had never known about! From then on, she was hooked. The World had come to her. It was a grand evening. . . .

Stella seemed less grand today. Burton had invited her to come out and board the barge for the big, big scene Liz, with her handmaidens, is doing today. The barge is way out at sea, never so golden in the sun, never so sumptuously decorated and peopled. It is a thing of perfect beauty to mark the moment when she sails into Tarsus to meet Antony. Well, we were late to see the best of it: not only the scene, but the in-fighting that was going on with everybody's nerves under strain—Mank, WW, Merman, Shamroy, the whole crowd. Golda went on early, but Madame Adler delayed me so that we finally had to go out in a petrifying rowboat, and if we had sunk—which I thought we were going to, inevitably—nobody would have known (for a while) because we were obscured by the varicolored smoke pots being used aboard the ship throwing billowing pink and blue smoke at us. All too mad. Once on board, I couldn't think of anything but the treacherous path back. That and the glaring heat. I saluted Elizabeth for carrying on in the heaviest of costumes—Irene Sharaff explained to me they were designed in midwinter to be shot in the spring, but here we are almost in July—without a bitch.

When I left to go back to the office, shooting was still going on, but from all indications the scene—a breath-taking one on the screen, I am sure—should be finished. At this point I am furious because my concern these past two days has been with getting out a story on Taylor finishing on this picture today. As a stockholder, I think we're entitled to know that. There's discussion about her working another day or so back at Torre Astura when we return to Rome, but in effect finishing with her at Ischia means at long last everybody can breathe easier; the worst is over, the best is yet to come. Well, it seems that Doc Merman had promised Elizabeth there would be no formal announcement that she is finished here, and Merman in turn asked Levathes to confirm that this info would be sealed (I saw Merman's letters to Pete). Merman tells Pete that Liz took the news gracefully and joked about her "closing notice." She said she wouldn't know what to do with herself now (I knew everybody acted as though this picture had become a way of life, going from England to Hollywood to Rome to Egypt to Hollywood and then maybe starting back and going all over again), but asked that it not be announced for fear that it would bring down Sybil.

So today we sit on the news that Liz is doing her last work on *Cleo* after how many years and how many deaths? Except of course for the fact that Joe wants to use her at least for a day or two back at Torre Astura. He's been in touch with Rosenman, who seems to hold the ultimate power today, by phone and cable, and the Judge seems to have agreed he can use her for that length of time if he can make a deal with her—I guess that means she doesn't get paid while she sits around Ischia waiting for the others to finish here before going back to Rome to finish up there. Still up in the air—one moment on, the next off—is Egypt, but that of course doesn't require Taylor, so it's a lesser problem.

Back at our office at the Jolly—which is the euphemism of all time—we have now had ten days of work work work the like of which I've never known, and the thought that we are between a bar and a swimming pool is misleading.

The swimming pool is misleading anyway. From what Golda and Sheila tell me, the Italians, in this resort for their health, like the water in the pool changed three times a week. As they only use natural boiling hot-springs water, each time they refill it it takes two days for it to cool enough so that you will not be boiled alive when you enter it. The girls refer to it as the boiling pool. . . .

As of today, Mank feels he needs until July 7 here in Ischia, with the second unit staying on here behind us to wrap up the Battle of Actium, while the first unit finishes up back in Rome and then proceeds to Egypt. But those revised-upward-again dates may not reflect the next Fox moves: Will July 1 be the new day the money stops? Will the June 27 meeting change things? Keep tuned in; or, we'll be listening.

Love,
Nathan

Ischia, June 27

Dear Jack,

Is today the day that will live in history? I am writing at lunchtime, it is 10 A.M. in New York and presumably the meeting is on. I am like a compulsive killer who cannot refrain from revisiting the scene; I know I must hear from you today (tonight) and there's little point in my writing, but I can't help myself. For one thing I have a letter from a well-placed friend (c a n 't say who) telling me that SPS will be out at today's meeting! Also that he foresees a small releasing company only to handle inventory (including *Cleopatra*) and otherwise a liquidation of Fox. To my mind it seems that this "small releasing company" could later become the nucleus of a new Fox, handling—for distribution—other indie product. And eventually back into prod'n, and so on. If SPS is booted out today, as this says, who is the successor? Not Levathes surely, not Michel who's failed his chance to show what he can do, Moskowitz with him, not DFZ according to the Abel Green story in June 20 *Variety*. Who then? Not Charlie, eh? So, Max Y.? Here they say Pete itches for the job and seems to think he has a chance. Is SPS's health a factor if they succeed in getting him out today?

I've also had a letter from Wald denying that *Ulysses* is tabled until 1963, but admitting it's a little unclear out there and I suppose today's events may clarify. Wanger has heard that SPS will be out as of today *but* that he is still going to put up a struggle, and if he manages to hold on again five of the board of directors are going to resign.

Wanger's line, by the way, now is that as his company and Taylor's are partners, they will sue Fox if necessary and force Fox out rather than let Fox stop the picture before it is finished. *Cleopatra's* taking the rap for years of Fox absurdity is really the dramatic climax, is it not? Of course, Walter rather ignores that Wanger's and Taylor's companies are the partners with only the small percentages.

Isn't it incredible when you think where Fox would be today if not for *Cleopatra*, and this company has, in its moment of crisis, the one magic power of restoration—and this very power is what it may endanger. Don't they know this is the biggest picture ever made?

For me personally the most incredible thing is the realization that after thirteen years of it, and six or seven years of feeling close to it, and two or three of feeling very close to it, I am away today when finally it looks as though *it* is happening.

Allow me to repeat a theme, but I think it's so shocking that Taylor's finishing on the picture here wasn't allowed to go out as news. I stood there helplessly, like an idiot, when she came off the barge—this was additional stuff on the waterfront at Ischia Ponte, showing the beautiful barge passing in front of the multitudes, and thus carried her another working day beyond what I thought earlier would be her last day—and I knew that she had participated in her last shot, but we didn't even have a photograph of The Moment. She came along the edge of the pier, I helped her into Joe's little launch tied up at the pier, she kissed Joe (who had Hollis Alpert and me on board for an interview that day), went into the cabin presumably to use the john, came out and went off. She seemed understandably melancholy and later, I hear, cried. Surely the picture of Liz kissing Joe on his finishing her last scheduled shot for *Cleopatra* is a news picture that would have broken round the world.

Speaking of kissing, now those Taylor-Burton kissing shots that were long-lensed over Bert Stern's shoulder are turning up in all the big weekly Italian mags. There can be little doubt that some of the local on-the-picture Italians are in cahoots with the *paparazzi*, or else how could they be stationed and positioned just right, knowing where the day's activity is to be and what to aim for?

Let me confess, with Taylor finishing on Monday and the big meeting in N.Y. today, Golda and I goofed off yesterday—with Erna, who has lately arrived from Rome and wanted to show us this country she's known and loved for a long time. We took the early-morning boat to Naples, then rented a car for the day which took us on the Amalfi Drive with a first stop at a fantastic villa near Ravello. Friends of Erna's live there, and we were given a tour of an elaborate retreat by another guest who was tending the gardens and hosing the lawn—he turned out to be Van Heflin.

Later we lunched at the most beautiful hotel on a terrace high above what looked like the world but must have been the beaches along the Amalfi—and still later we stopped at Amalfi, and finally at Positano which was breath-taking in approach but turned out to be very Provincetown-like in person and quite a disappointment. Home again last night (home being Ischia now) after a great day, the first true vacation day in the two months I've been in Italy. Crossing back by slow steamer just at and after sunset, Naples looked as beautiful at last as one has always heard—the black silhouette of coastline fading, fading away until at last it was the sea itself—and I think now I will see all of Italy in a new light. Had it been like this when Golda and I were here ten years ago? Had we been too young to really appreciate it? Now it is to savor. . . .

Nathan

■■■■■■■■■■■■

WEISS   ISCHIA   JUNE 27
SKOURAS RESIGNED STOP WILL STAY ON UNTIL REPLACE-
MENT IS FOUND BY COMMITTEE CONSISTING OF KEY BOARD
MEMBERS AND HIMSELF STOP LETTER FOLLOWS LOVE
BRODSKY

■■■■■■■■■■■■

Dear Nat,

Just dashed off a cable, and now to recap a little of what it's been like. It's been the week in which *it* happened all right and in which I've not been able to write all the background of the events, the meetings, conversations, etc.

The committee to look into a Skouras successor, now that he has resigned, consists of SPS himself, the Judge, Gould, Clarkson, Lehman and Loeb. That looks favorable for The Boat's side, I guess. It seems that while Aubrey and Youngstein are candidates, they are looking for other candidates as well.

They got rid of SPS first and then, having done what they were almost surprised they were able to accomplish, they are setting out to find a successor. Gould talked to Aubrey and SPS to Youngstein, before the meeting today, but no one has had a formal offer. So they need names. I planted two. The first is Si Fabian. The second, SCE. Apart from our personal friendship with Fabian, we have long felt he would be the ideal theater man with a production mind and the confidence of the whole industry to support him in taking over the company. As for Charlie, we have realized for some time now that he is the best qualified man within the organization —the only one in fact who knows production, knows distribution, is the ad-pub dean of them all, and apart from the colorful personal hell he has caused us and those who went before us from time to time, what would any of us be or any of us know without him? I am told the reaction to those suggestions has been one of surprise and favor, so we shall see.

Last Friday there was a meeting at the Skouras club, the Metropolitan Club I mean, which was crucial. *Variety* got the story over the weekend and ran the story that really broke it in Monday's daily on the Coast. (Clip sent.) On Monday word spread as it does from West to East within the hours of the time change. Everybody started calling and speculating about the imminent upheaval. But nothing really counted much until the *Times* did something about it in print today.

As of the meeting today no one was really certain as to how it would all come out. At 9:15 the office was crowded with half a dozen reporters, AP, UPI, photographers, etc. The meeting began at 9:30 and although I told the press people they were foolish to wait in our office so long, it would take all day, they wanted to stay. At lunch time, we ordered from the Stage for the dozen or more who were there.

By 3:30 or so, we have every reporter in town here, including of course all the trades and *Time* magazine. By now we had liquor and coffee sent in. Then I got a call to come down and see Charlie.

I find him in Skouras' outer office while the meeting is apparently taking some kind of break. When Charlie ducks back into the boardroom, I see a couple of guys congratulating Gould, one of them saying, "Well, Milton, you've really done it." Then Charlie comes out with the announcement and shows it to me and says, "Go up and give this to them, and tell them there will be no press conference and the meeting will go to about eight." I said, "Charlie, please, you're a vice-president (I finally said it), it should be you who talks to them." He paused a minute, gulped, and said okay. So upstairs we go, and in the office mobbed with reporters and photographers, Charlie reads the statement while the bulbs pop in his face and he gets paler.

One of the reporters says, "Mr. Einfeld, how did the vote go? What members were for him or against him?" Charlie hemmed and hawed, cleared his throat and was about to say something, when I stepped in and said, "There was no vote. How could there be a vote? The man just resigned."

Later, with Levathes in his office, Charlie bounded up from behind his desk to shake my hand and proclaim what a fast thinker I was and how I saved him. Levathes asked what happened and Charlie told him, painting a great PR portrait of me. So if Levathes stays, maybe he won't always hate me.

Still later, Charlie tells me that when SPS gave him the statement of his resignation to announce, he said, "Congratulations, I guess you're happy now." This hurt Charlie badly. As he sat there shaking his head, I told him I had always felt his allegiance in that direction was never appreciated. Charlie said, "Well, you do something like that because you feel it inside. When you give the beggar the dime, it's not because you want something from the beggar."

That's about it. As for a further analysis of the situation, your guess is as good as mine. I understand that the meeting was as bloody as anything ever has been and that most of the board threatened to resign if SPS didn't quit. Finally, I gather, Rosenman prevailed upon the old man to look at the handwriting on the wall.

As before,
Jack

■■■■■■■■■■■■

Dear Jack,

A quick line to say thanks for the first batch of clips, your letter, cable, etc. Charlie made no contact at all. As far as he is concerned, we would have first learned the news from the phone calls by the wire services, asking for comment on Skouras' resignation, if it were not for you.

The most interesting correspondence I know about these past few days has been going on between Mankiewicz and Rosenman. The last cable Joe sent off to the Judge, to which he has not yet had a response, told the Judge that his previous cable must have been misunderstood or mistransmitted to draw the response it did. It's gotten so hot and heavy on the cable that Joe has Rosemary [Matthews, production assistant] take his copy over to Naples each morning on the early boat and send it from there, as he doesn't trust the transmission here.

The question is still the work to be done before going to Egypt. It seems that Egypt itself is no problem, as the financing for Egypt was given by Fox to one of the partnership corporations long ago, so they have the money. They plan to start July 15 for about ten days there, but I expect it will be delayed a week or so, especially if everything else is completed beforehand, including Pharsalia. I still think the picture can be finished properly by August 1.

Joe needs the girl one day at Torre Astura, but there are ramifications to the studio's telling *him* to make a deal that make a long, interesting story. Like captains at sea, we met in respective motor launches, coming and going from the shore to one of the barges out at sea, and across the roar of motors we shouted and tried to hear each other.

One thing I hear all right. That is, that if Mank isn't allowed to do what he must do, then he has told them he quits. In fact, the tense of his cable made it clear: he has already quit, if they don't come to their senses. So here we have a director who has resigned and a producer who has been fired; yet both keep working, as witness the frantically rushing circumstances in which the matter was discussed. It's a farce!

Now, as I must go, just a sentence to say tell all my friends at 42nd Street that my chagrin at being here this moment is overwhelming. Having thrived on and enjoyed so many near-climaxes, it is ironic not to be present at the real one. Don't you agree now that you got the better half of this year's deal?

Love,
Nat

■■■■■■■■■■■■

New York, July 3

Dear Nat,

It's my birthday, and I have to work. Isn't that sad? You'd think you'd have remembered. Bob and Sheila remembered. They sent a card. You'd think you'd have sent a card. You'd think you would have told Dick Hanley so Elizabeth could've sent me a loving birthday message. Oh, well, I guess you just don't love me any more.

So today's pre-Independence Day lecture was on *money*. Charlie spent yesterday afternoon in a Rosenman-chaired exec committee meeting and said they want him to cut and *now*. He says the Art Department *must go* this time and he sounds like he means it.

You have probably seen the clips on the Zanuck fuss by now. Do you think maybe the Zanuck statement was Hift-written? It seemed to include all the quotes we ever said to Fred. Of course it may be that those are all the obvious points that nobody ever dared make before; anyway it's eloquent. I would've called, but I figured I'd better cool it. Zanuck gets here on Thursday and will maybe call—certainly I'll call if anything big happens.

I'm off to a birthday dinner at my mother's—not even a note from you even—and a relaxed 4th at home tomorrow. Have I told you lately that I miss you? It's been that kind of day.

Jack

Dear Jack,

It is eight o'clock in the morning on this glorious American holiday which we are not celebrating here. In this dawn's early light I find the only time to write you. We are traveling back to Rome late today, the first unit follows tomorrow, and we will resume shooting back there—at the Torre Astura location—the next day.

Yesterday morning, sitting with Walter and with Golda on the breakfast terrace outside my office, with all the clips on last week back in New York, we vicariously lived through The Day. Added to that is the spice of Zanuck's eloquent blast from Paris. God, his statement is magnificent and needed saying just that way—unforgettable; I've wired Hift to say so.

I talked to Earl Wilson on the phone last night in response to his cabled query re Mank getting permission to shoot more with Taylor (he did not); Earl told me he can't get any information in N.Y. It's all a round robin. He asks Einfeld for some info, Einfeld tells him to try Rosenman, he tries, Rosenman tells him to try Levathes, he does, Levathes tells him to try Einfeld, he starts over.

Biggest of today's pieces of news—other than that they won't signal to Mank that he can do the necessary day or two with Liz back in Rome, which will be a calamity, he thinks—is that Egypt is out. It seems that the Egyptians tried to shake us down for more money after the deal was made, so Hollywood will have to substitute for Egypt. Of course the whole company, so many of them from the Coast, couldn't be more delighted that everybody and everything will have to be transported back there for finishing. As Nanni says, can you see him and Nella in Arizona?

Sunday we took our last jaunt around Ischia, which I have come to love. I love it down at the old castle at the Ponte—where the whole damn island population turned out one night to watch some night shooting with the barge—and at the primitive but marvelous pasta-and-fish-for-$2 restaurant down there; I love it at the port of Ischia itself with one of those great European color-and-light skylines at sunset; I even love it driving in the dawn hours up to the fashionable Lacco Ameno; I love most of all the little cliff village of Forio, which time seems to have passed by since the Spanish invaders left it; I love the little town at the tip of Ischia called San

Angelo which at this and other off seasons becomes a German tourist colony and is probably the lowest-cost holiday in the Western world; and I love the Regina Isabella, which is probably close to the highest. And, if you will permit me, I love Our Cove.

It was there we spent yesterday afternoon, Golda and I, up on the Ischian beach eating from the production lunchboxes (excellent) prepared for the crew, while our *Cleo* chauffeur waited for hours for us to get properly tanned in our near-private cove under the timeless Ischian rocks. (Oh, those board of directors people would die, the way we wasted money—tens of dollars—in Ischia.) That was our farewell to Ischia—a half-day payoff for nearly three weeks of round-the-clock work, and damn near worth it.

I thought my friend Larry Willig's remark to me in a letter about the-end-of-Skouras singularly appropriate; I agree with what he says completely.

"Now that Spyros has been kicked upstairs, I don't feel very much like making my usual jokes. It seems a shame that we can't walk away from success at the Top. And that we always have to be pushed. There's something so undignified about that, so grubby, that it makes all men smaller and less, less what?"

Love,
Nathan

WEISS   ROME   JULY 6
IT LOOKS LIKE MUSTACHE WITH ZEUS AS PLANKHEAD RE-
GARDS BRODSKY

BRODSKY   NEW YORK   JULY 6
YOUR LAST CABLE SEEMS GARBLED STOP UNABLE DECIPHER
COMPLETELY ALTHOUGH GUESS MUSTACHE SYNONYM FOR
THREE TIME IRVING THALBERG AWARD WINNER BEST WEISS

WEISS   ROME   JULY 7
YOU DOPE STOP OF COURSE MUSTACHE ZANUCK STOP NOW
MUST RISK WORLD KNOWING BECAUSE YOU NEVER
WATCHED CAPTAIN MIDNIGHT AND GOT DECODER RING
STOP PLANKHEAD TO FOLLOW DISGUSTEDLY JACK

■■■■■■■■■■■■

Dear Jack,

Well, we're back in Rome—and it's hot. When I went down from our apartment this morning, I passed the porter on my way to the waiting car to take me to the studio. He handed me a cable which I can't figure out; too cryptic. Zanuck is mustache, of course, but Zeus "plankhead" must have been a typo.

I went down to Torre Astura this morning, in the heat and the dust, with Bert Stern to do his bidding now that he's returned to try to finish off his photo story. The pix of Burton and Taylor in costume are complicated by a) the costumes and makeup have been packed up to ship home and b) with Taylor now off the picture, and their refusing to let Mank work the day he needs with her here, I have no right to ask her to pose. But Bert asked her and she's willing if we can unlock the costumes, so we're trying.

Also had a call from Sheilah Graham. She's coming back to Rome, and, having treated Richard fairly when she interviewed him last time, wants to try to line up Elizabeth this time. I trudged down to the beach on the Mediterranean coast where Liz was sunning and swimming with Dickie between his takes on the pic (of course she's not working and is only around as an observer), and interrupted them to ask her if she would go for Sheilah. She was right to the point. Richard, per usual, added his very profound "all press are dangerous" as far as they are concerned. But I tried.

As you might have predicted, today the word is that someone has gotten the Egyptians to cooperate again, along the lines originally laid down, and so we are going to Egypt after all! About a week from now. We finished down at Torre Astura today (they were still working when I left) and Monday night we will have our last shooting here at Cinecittà, a night shot. If Pharsalia comes through, that will be done in a mountain location out of Cinecittà before we head off to Egypt. But today's the last day for Mank to be able to make the shot of Taylor crossing to and entering her Alexandrian tomb, so I guess in the finished picture we'll have to find her there without ever knowing how she got there, because the shambles of Fox all these long years finally culminates in their forbidding this detail to be filmed. It is truly incredible, or have I said that? A cable came to Joe saying: "Levathes refuses to reconsider Taylor scenes and Pharsalia too expensive." So I think they've struck out—unless Rex Harrison can persuade 20th they're a charity case and get them to accept his offer to finance the Pharsalia sequence himself!

Don't give up the barge, however. Martin Gang (Liz's attorney), Greg Bautzer (WW's attorney), and Charlie Feldman (JLM's agent) are all due tomorrow and will meet Sunday night with Joe, WW, Taylor and Burton for a *last try*. They look a little furtive while making their plans. Has any creative group on any film or play ever been so tightly bound together in a just cause before? None of the usual director-producer or star rivalries enter into it at all. Talk about a dedicated foursome. Actually Richard and Joe don't belong in on the conference, only Taylor and Wanger being the partners, but Wanger and Liz insist they be in on it for "artistic support." I'd love to be in on it—if only for moral support—but needless to say won't be. It's a hell of a way to finish any picture, let alone this one, with your lawyers fighting the company to let you!

After the mad four-hour scramble to unpack Elizabeth's wigs and costumes and having a car rush them down to TA, she wouldn't pose—wasn't in the mood. It's now slated for Monday afternoon at Cinecittà, before Burton's night work on the final Philippi scene here.

Called Sheilah back in Venice; despite her generous offer, I told her, Liz says no dice. Sheilah is coming on Wednesday anyhow; she's sure there's a story here.

Did I ever tell you how sorry I was about missing your birthday? I mean, don't think this is tongue-in-cheek. I love you and your birthday and your wife and your dog and expect to love your child.

I know I had something else on my mind. Ah, yes. Sheilah G. has a story that Burton has a bid for the Lerner show; I spoke to Richard about it and he says it is premature as not a song is written yet. But Richard Burton in the new musical by Alan Jay Lerner and Richard Rodgers! With Barbara Harris yet! (Oops, there goes Elizabeth Taylor.)

Wald writes that *Ulysses* is off, pending Peter Sellers, to April '63; and why don't they consider him, at long last, to head the studio?

Will be waiting for the English translation on that Greek cable
—anxiously.

Love,
Nat

P.S. Have seen the first of the footage from Ischia (the huge
resplendent gold barge stuff) and it is glorious. Even Joe seems
pleased, and he is his toughest critic, as we know.

Must tell you one other story. Joe met with C. D. Jackson [pub-
lisher of *Life*] at the latter's request. I got a call from that very
bright young man, Bob Piser, they have here now (not sure he was
here when you were), asking if Mank would. How do you turn
down the publisher of *Life?* Obviously not, if you're a press agent;
but you do if you're a Mankiewicz. But I cajoled some, and Joe
agreed to meet for drinks. It turned out to be easy, because the
Jacksons are stopping at the Grand; so we arranged it for just after
Mank came home from the studio tonight. As soon as they met,
Joe's reticence evaporated, and that brilliant streak of mind-turn-
ing-into-words began to display itself.

He described Liz & Burton as not so much lovers as "two actors
who don't know how to get offstage" because there's been no script
writer around to show them how. He used this to illustrate his
thesis that these people only know about life from what they have
read in their scripts.

I do think Joe is off to this extent. It's obvious that once Liz
finished on the picture, Burton could have dumped her and
brought back Sybil. The crazy idea that he was just holding onto
her to guarantee that the picture got finished doesn't hold any
more. I no longer know whether to believe all those who smugly
assert that Burton always goes home to Sybil.

Jackson, looking a little like Bennett Cerf, was most gracious.
He was joined by two young *Time*n or *Time*types and eventually
by the publisher's lady. Joe seemed smitten with them, and told
them everything, I mean *everything*. About the scandals, the romance, the Egyptian situation, Fox vs. the artists on "finishing,
but not completing the picture" (making the distinction), and just
about every inside bit of dirt there's been. Nor did Joe hold back
on his resentments against *Time-Life*. He says they even panned

All About Eve, which nobody else did. Can that be true? He cutely mocked the *Time*types who kept calling Mr. Jackson "C. D." And he told Jackson he was sure there's a young fairy at *Time* who has already made all the puns for a piece on *Cleopatra* and has them in cold storage.

And—this part I berated him on especially, afterwards—he kept telling Jackson it would be a better picture if Fox hadn't forced him to write it off the cuff, cut it short before he's finished, etc. I told him this sounds like every director who tries to shift the blame for a lousy picture. He says he's trying to win a climate of support in the press for the underdog artist vs. the ruthless moneymen. But I don't think he needs that; I think that is superfluous.

Love,

N.W.

Dear Jack,

The "Big 4" summit meeting has come and gone, and there is very little information to be had. Whether they made contact with New York I don't know. This much we do know: the last, the very last filming here at Cinecittà, took place tonight—some battle footage with Burton. Liz held court under a tent to one side, as best one could see in the flickering torchlight. It was all very colorful, and quite late at night—we just now got home—it was once and for all ended at Cinecittà. No tears, and very little demonstration.

Maybe this was a Big 4 achievement: we are to do two days in the hills for Pharsalia, so the picture will have some kind of abbreviated opening at least. And then, maybe by week's end, to Egypt. Will let you know.

Best,
Nat

■■■■■■■■■■■■

New York, July 9

Dear Nat,

Can't believe you aren't really putting me on in your letter and cables. My cable of course referred to Zanuck as "the mustache" for president, with Skouras, the head Greek (Zeus) as "plankhead" which is shorthand for chairman-of-the-board. Board. Plank. Get it? That's the way it looked, and still does to some eyes as a matter of fact. But nothing solid developed, and so we shall have to wait. Zanuck departed for Paris over the weekend, after apparently getting nowhere with the board, and I think the attached *Wall Street Journal* story sums up the situation as well as anything I could say.

As before,
Jack

■■■■■■■■■■■■

Dear Jack,

Had a real knock-down drag-out (as he would say) with Charlie on the phone yesterday, in which he forbids me and Nella (who being Egyptian originally speaks Arabic and would be invaluable to me) to go to Egypt when the company departs at the end of the week! I guess he's terrified about authorizing anyone in his department to spend the money to fly to Egypt. I don't see how it affects or saves anything else. If it's criticism he fears—that criticism at any rate—surely he's open to as much, more, I think, for *not* having us covered in Egypt. I was outraged on the phone, but have rather coolly accepted it. It just seems incredible to me that *Cleopatra* is going to Egypt, where the production's vulnerability to press scandal far exceeds anything we have known in Italy, I gather, without an official spokesman. Charlie says scornfully that Walter Wanger can handle the press there, having nothing better to do. They say the censorship is rough, and communications may be nil. I'm in doubt about the possibility of phone calls, or the likelihood of uncensored cables.

We will operate the press office from here through the ten days to two weeks now scheduled for Egypt, and hope to be able to get in enough information to have news to send out. After all, this is to be the last phase of our "climax on climax" publicity, and presumably the best kind we can get, as it proves to the world that *Cleopatra* at last is finished.

Walter promises to cable daily, and Bob Penn will slip me some letters with background info. Roddy McDowall has also been designated a spy, and promises to get the word out and back to me. So if we hear nothing, we'll pretty much know that it's being stopped. But can you glean how totally unthinkable it is to me that 20th will have no responsible voice (me) to issue news or handle the ticklish public relations situation there? And this after visas were obtained, and everything put in order for going there. One more small detail typical of *Cleopatra.*

Love,

Nat

Dear Nat,

Before anything else, I have to tell you biggest personal story. Bill Stutman [Fox publicist] got me an interview for a TV show called "Password" which is a word game whereby two celebrities (male and female) and two contestants (male and female) play five times a week for half an hour. I won't go into the game, but it's five days a week on the CBS TV network. So I pass two interviews and yesterday afternoon the guy calls me and tells me to come over—I'm on that afternoon!

I go over and appear on a show which is taped for viewing on Friday, July 20. The celebs were Richard Hayes and Lillian Roth and I won $300. Can you imagine? Plus a portable record player. I still can't believe it and can't wait to see the damned thing next Friday at 2 P.M. when all the boys will traipse up to Dick Brooks's pad to view the thing. Should be one of the all-time howls. Can't tell you what a fantastic experience. I may now try and get my own show. Can you imagine? Three hundred bucks. It's much easier than working here.

We saw *Sodom and Gomorrah* the other day and it is terrible, just what you think it will be. I was going to call The Boat and tell him about it the day the board was voting on it, but thought better of meddling. Anyway, it looks as if we'll get it, Charlie rooting for it strongest of all. I said it would be worth one million and Charlie said, "It's a million-two." So I said, "All right, for a million-two I won't quibble," and then he says, "And, of course, you guarantee to spend a million for prints and advertising." Then we started arguing over how much it had to do in order to break even, and he tells me that we'll be getting a distrib fee from the first buck and this will at least bring some weekly revenue in, etc. From that point of view, I guess he's got something. I guess I just don't want to be part of a company which distributes that kind of film. What hope is there for this company when they can buy *Sodom and Gomorrah*?

To jump around: Irene Sharaff is back. I've spoken to her and we hope she'll do some work for us. She said she will, sounded very nice and anxious to make up for some of the sordid publicity. . . . Charlie says cuts here coming soon. Five story-department people let go today. Art department should be next. (This sounds like last memo from guy awaiting H-bomb rays. Who knows? . . .

Looks tonight as if Monroe movie is being reactivated with same cast, director, etc. Mistake?

The Boat says Gould won't let go on Levathes, he is their man, and that Zanuck won't win a proxy fight (MG says "he has as much chance as a snowball in hell"). I think a compromise might be Arnold Grant and some other Zanuckite on board, with PL as president. Board meets on the 25th, and we'll see. During the whole Monroe firing hassle, our department has been pretty much out of it. However, yesterday I was told Monroe had agreed to make a public apology, for which we would take her back and start the film again. I was asked, very confidentially, to write the apology for her, and so I locked myself in and wrote one. I wrote a moderate one, one in which she might apologize but save face. They took me off the assignment.

Got to go now. Love, love.

Jack

Dear Jack,

So stunned by learning at 8 this morning from a phone call by one of the wire service people of Jerry Wald's death. The awful symmetry of the death of this one bit of animation in the studio is overwhelming. I had a letter from him, written Monday of this week, which came the day before yesterday. Under the sad circumstances, let me quote from it.

"Right now, the studio is filled with chaos, confusion, contradictions and just plain old-fashioned crap. I wish they would settle the presidency so we can all go back to work. As far as I am concerned, I wish Zanuck would get the job because he's the only one who has the energy, the initiative, the respect—and, most of all—stock, to push everything through that should be pushed through. The great tragedy here at Fox is not so much the pictures we made but the pictures that we didn't make. Will go into a longer discourse on this in my next letter.

"The publicity continues to build on *Cleopatra*. I don't think anything has been heralded with such fanfare, except, of course, the coming of Christ. How can I put the two of them in the same category, except that Taylor, like Mary Magdalene, is being stoned, and I refer to the words of JC when he said: 'Let you without sin cast the first stone.' I rest my case..

"Please tell Walter to take it easy. Ulcers are not becoming to producers.

Warmly,
Jerry"

He worries about Wanger's health. And refers to his next letter, and of course there isn't going to be a next letter. And I feel rotten.

As I indicated early in the week when it first looked that way, Fox gave in on Pharsalia (done) and the Mausoleum (not done, for complicated reasons), so there will be no suit pressed by the Wanger & Taylor companies against Fox. As I said, I guess this was a victory for the meeting of last Sunday night. In the end it may be that the difficulties of *Cleopatra* throughout the chaotic period of the Fox empire-in-decline, wildly looking for a scapegoat and mindful as any falling empire would be of Rome as the logical place to find one, was annoying to *Cleo* but not fatal. Fox couldn't kill *Cleo*; it remains to be seen whether *Cleo*, by its staggering cost, kills Fox. I don't think it will; I think we are right to continue to think that *Cleo*, on the contrary, will be its greatest triumph. But it is a good business-world illustration, the best we are likely to know at first hand, of what desperate harm desperate men can do. My boy, let this be a lesson to you.

Pharsalia was done, by the way, but I'm not sure how well. We had just the two days up on location in the hills, and probably insufficient time to prepare for it. The picture will open after the battle with just the dead (men and horses) strewn around the battlefield. Burton and Harrison (I had not seen him work before since the day of the Procession which now seems like years ago, he having come back just for this) were on horse most of the time. I went up to see it. Sheilah Graham is back to close off a series of visits to *Cleopatra* almost as perennial as the picture itself, and I invited her up for this "last chance," but she declined the rocky-road trip up there. It was a treacherous two or three hours and very little worth seeing, except of course for me it was the last day of *Cleopatra* filming I shall ever see, inasmuch as I'm not going to Egypt. Offstage there was a moment or two with Elizabeth visiting Burton on the set. Do you get the feeling this is the end of a long, long run; like the seventh year of *Tobacco Road* or something, and everyone is going through the motions of something they have been tired of doing for ages and ages but can't seem to help themselves from repeating?

Sheilah, Walter, Golda and I did have a thoroughly nice dinner at Flavia's—Tullio Carminati stopped by, or are you too young to know what that meant to me?—and Sheilah got a splendid interview with Walter, who has scarcely talked to anyone else, so again she gets something out of her *Cleopatra* stop that nobody else got.

That's all for now.

Best,
Nathan

WEISS   ROME   JULY 16
NOW THAT ROME PHASE ALMOST OVER LET ME SAY YOU
HAVE DONE YOUR JOB TOO WELL STOP ITS SO QUIET STOP
AM BEGINNING TO MISS THE GOOD OLD DAYS OF TAYLOR-
BURTON HIJINX STOP MAYBE YOU HAVE GONE TOO FAR STOP
ALL THE DRAMA IS HERE BUT WHERE OH WHERE IS THE
COMEDY QUESTIONINGLY BRODSKY

BRODSKY   NEW YORK   JULY 17
VERY SIMPLE STOP AS SAM BEHRMAN ONCE SAID THIS IS NO
TIME FOR COMEDY STOP THEY SEEM TO HAVE SETTLED
DOWN LIKE ANY GOOD OLD MARRIED COUPLE STOP STOP
QUIBBLING STOP CANT YOU APPRECIATE THE HANDIWORK
OF A MASTER REGARDS WEISS

Rome, July 21

Dear Jack,

Haven't heard from you and assume you are sweating it out until the meeting next week—which should decide all. Is Zanuck on or off these days as the likeliest contender for the presidency?

Very little word has come seeping back to us from Egypt. A postcard from Roddy, who got to see the Pyramids in Cairo before going on to Alexandria, but I take it as significant that nothing but a "tourist" note got through. The first I heard from Egypt was from AP when Burton made a statement upon arriving there that, contrary to our announcement, Taylor has *not* finished and has scenes to do in Egypt which she will do as soon as she gets her visa and comes there. Of course this is untrue and she has no scenes there, but apparently this is his way of trying to cover for her expected joining him there—as though she will be there for work. Here we sit between New York and Egypt, unable to do our jobs because New York forbids us to spend a couple of hundred dollars to go to Egypt, and in Cairo we have censors who don't permit open communication. I have just given up in deference to the heat, boredom, lack of energy and general confusion. We do know from a Wanger cable that, true to Nella's prediction, the company was not met properly in Cairo and given their visas there on arrival (as they were supposed to be), so they had to sit it out at the airport and the production got started a day late. Roddy, and I don't know who else, traveled separately and apparently had no difficulty.

I am enclosing a recent *L'Europeo* with a story on our sometime stills photographer, Tazio, as "king of the *paparazzi*." Maybe, as Nella says, he's a former king—and legit now. But, in view of all our grief, isn't it odd that for so many months he worked for us! Forgive me for sounding like Nixon, but I think this is a charge which can be leveled at your administration, Mr. Kennedy.

Current prognosis is that the *Cleopatra* last patrol will straggle back here late next week. Just the key people. Most of the Hollywoodites will go directly back home from Egypt. But isn't there a dramatic irony afoot in that *Cleopatra* will finally come to the end of her road just about the same day that a new life is in the offing for dear old 20th? Keep in touch.

Nathan

161

Dear Nat,

Have your letter of Saturday, and apologize for the non-writing of the past week. But, as you suspected, it's been a week of waiting for the volcano to hot, and I think this week the lava will start spilling over. It's been so hectic, and the pattern keeps changing every day. I am staying in at lunch now, mostly to write this.

Zanuck is here of course and it seems that he and SPS—after all these years of doing battle—have joined forces to vote Zanuck in on Wednesday. With Louis Nizer in the act, it seems as though they have corralled enough board strength, but Loeb, Gould and Rosenman (who obviously would be out of a job if DFZ is prez and Skouras his chairman of the board) aren't being counted out by The Boat's faction. Wednesday will be crucial.

The rumors fly on both sides. I heard, for instance, that Howard Hughes was quite ready to step in and "help out by taking over" prior to the proxy fight threat, but that now seems to fade in the distance. More current is the word that Loeb and Zanuck had a confrontation in which DFZ was challenged on the basis of the production record of his independent company releasing through Fox.

Meanwhile we're getting our publicity activity on Zanuck for *The Longest Day* confused with Zanuck's campaign for the presidency, and Charlie is in a hot seat from which there is no easy escape. If you sit in it, you burn. The press won't show for his announcements of charity premières on the picture at this point, unless he's also going to talk about the upcoming board meeting. Finally, I got the word from Charlie: "Invite all the press; I've talked to Zanuck and he'll talk about the Fox situation." I sent out a guarded wire to this effect, which prompted the *Wall Street Journal* to check it out with The Boat, who called me, boiling, accusing the corporation of using its employees to hold Zanuck in a favorable light for a proxy fight. Apparently the ethics or rules of the game preclude building up Zanuck ostensibly for one activity when he's running for office, another activity. It's something like electioneering too close to the polls.

Charlie goes white when I tell him about this and, a bit later, tells me, "Zanuck won't talk." I looked at him steely-eyed, because

I had warned him of this to begin with; but what's he to do when he is forced to try to play in everybody's game? The Boat phoned back, pleased that the press turnout for DFZ would now be small, now that we were forced to send out another wire saying Zanuck would hold forth only on *The Longest Day*.

Now Charlie wants to have a Skouras press conference this week to announce that *Cleopatra* is over at week's end. Though I tell him he's heading into trouble again, he can't hear of it—probably because now SPS is demanding a display of partisanship. It's been that kind of a week—insane. Will let you know as soon as anything breaks.

Love,
Jack

WEISS   ROME   JULY 25
AS EXPECTED LOVE BRODSKY

■■■■■■■■■■■■

Dear Nat,

Well, it's the day after the Big Day and I have some sort of semblance of things now, and even though it's late at night and I'm
home, dead, I'll try to go over everything.

It became apparent early this week that DFZ and SPS had lined
up all the votes, Lehman being the key, save for Gould, Loeb and
Rosenman. Yesterday at four P.M. the board meeting started, after
a preliminary meeting of the committee to choose the president.
Charlie had told me there would definitely be an announcement
at the end of the meeting, but around 4:30 reports began to filter
in that Louis Nizer had told the press that there would be a press
conference at 6 P.M. in his office. We deduced that this meant they
were going to be deadlocked and would announce a proxy fight.
How wrong we were.

There began, around this time, a series of six or seven phone
calls between The Boat and myself. He at first sounded discour-
aged, then, when he thought a deadlock might be in the offing, he
told me, "I'll compromise on Koegel; see if you can get word to
Gould to call me." He even called Charlie and told him to tell
Gould, if he saw him, to call him. But it was all in vain.

All the press were standing by and at 7:45, when I was called
down, the announcements, mimeographed in advance by Nizer,
were given us and we passed them out. I took the photographers
into Skouras' office, where we took jubilant handshaking pix of
SPS and Our New Leader!

Today, Charlie was buoyant, telling me how great it would be
under Zanuck and how he could "talk to him." Charlie: "Zanuck
and I have the same relationship as you and I do, Jack. I yell at
him, tell him he's crazy, doesn't know what he's doing, and he
does the same with me, but underneath it all, there's a deep affection." He does seem cozy with Zanuck. Hift and I agreed his old
loyalties to Zanuck are more important than anything.

Today the resignations came from Gould, Loeb and Rosenman.
As for SPS wanting to hold the stage on announcing the end of
Cleopatra, DFZ simply told Charlie to tell Skouras he didn't want
him to have a press conference, and that was that. Do you think
we're getting a quick preview of things-to-come?

There you have it, and it should be this way until *The Longest Day* opens and Darryl can devote his time to the company. As for *Cleopatra*, it's said there's still talk about dividing it into two pix, which is like going back to the beginning or "This is where I came in." It's the only sure way to ruin it.

It's hard to believe that we've really come through this whole thing. It will be something to tell my son or daughter—when he or she grows up. For Dorothy, it was worth it just to go home in maternity clothes, and for me, well, I *think* it was worth it. Everyone at home is sure to say "What an experience," but with all the excitement of the film and what's happened, I'll probably never think of Rome without thinking of being awakened at 4:00 A.M. three nights a week to make an official statement about something I knew nothing about.

Did I ever tell you about the very last phone message I got before leaving Rome? It was from Bill Sunderland of UPI, and there on my desk was a note which said: "Mr. Sunderland called. He wants to know if you have any new denials."

Thanks for everything and love,

Jack

Dear Jack,

Your long and much appreciated letter arrived this morning. So
it's *Over* Over There. Well, it's *Over* Over Here, too. Today we're
finishing packing everything up, and later in the day it all goes to
the shippers to be transported back to dear old 444 West 56 Street,
Noo Yawk City. As the wire services have informed you, weary
Wanger, wheelchair-ridden Mank (he hurt his foot on the Egyptian sands), et al. have returned to Rome; Burton, too, but separately; and she was at the airport to meet him. But you know
what? I no longer cared; and because they are no longer working
on the picture and no longer any of our business, I didn't even see
them in. I did see Mankiewicz and Wanger in, however. How long
we had waited for that day. Back from Egypt, which meant they
had written *finis* at long long last to the costliest, most plagued,
most written and talked about, and most brilliant of all films.

We went back to the Grand, and had the warmth of a farewell
from Joe and a last drink with Walter, as impeccably ascot-tied on
the Egyptian sands I am sure as he is at the studio. They, and the
stature of their work-under-fire (Who knows? Maybe the fire
warmed their work; where can inspiration and greatness be where
there is no blaze?) will survive it all. But it is a luxury to know that
there will no longer be the need to run interference for Our Star.
As for Burton, he remains for me, to the end, cool, shrewd and
amiable, but I think I will prefer to remember him for his perform-
ances—this one, as Antony, and the one in *Camelot* in particular.
There have been no better in our time. Roddy is by far the nicest
—*and* superb in the film; so you *can* be both. Harrison I never
really knew; but his acting says it all. But the people, both for what
they are and for what they stand (and stood, if you want to go on
making jokes), who count in all this are Wanger and Mankiewicz.

I suppose it's because in my old movie-struck way it still matters
deeply to me that I became at least a little close to two of Hollywood's own, who are both masters and legends. And to have done
so in a time of crisis, crystallized by the very essence of that crisis
that you see in *Cleopatra*, is a piece of good luck that strikes me
almost as "fated." For surely *Cleopatra* will come to mark the end
of a Hollywood era—Hollywood as we knew it as kids, as the

world has come to have an image of it. I think with this film it can be seen that the whole system finally breaks down under its own weight. That genius has salvaged greatness out of bigness is an accident not likely to be repeated, or too soon attempted. If I were Max Lerner—a kind genius—I would let my insight and my sympathy flow. Or if I were David Riesman, I could with sociological detachment figure out the implications for our society and our culture. Being neither, and not adequate to the task, I find it for the moment enough to point out how fertile the ground is, and the certainty I feel about Our Year in Rome being researched and microscoped for its microcosm attributes in some year yet to come.

Do you feel (you must), as I do, a kind of what-are-you-going-to-do-after-the-war attitude? Somehow or other I don't think the Zanuck occupation will appeal to me. Admittedly I would like to see *Cleo* through at Fox, but that would be the only inducement. I think I will hold to my resolve that this is *it*. I know that you will too. And surely there has never been a more logical time, if you like neat dramatic constructions to apply in life as they do in art, for us to make the break. *Cleopatra* is over, and we have been close to it. The Skouras era, almost the company as we know it, is over at 20th Century-Fox, and with it comes a glimpse of the final THE END on the movies, as so many of us have lived them and dreamed them since childhood.

There will always be movies of course, and presumably better ones than there ever were before; and yet they won't quite be as grand, as foolish, as wonderful as they used to be. How marvelous that *Cleopatra*, the last of them, transcends them all! That, with *Cleopatra*, The Movies go out in style. I don't know who killed Cock Robin. Did Skouras do it to *Cleopatra*? (He damn near did, I suspect.) Did *Cleopatra* do it to Skouras? (I think the issue was phony, and it would have happened anyway, but who's to know?)

But, neatly, as in art sometimes and in life even less often, they came out together. It's been a fun ride right to the end of the line. I'm glad we hitched onto it, but this circus wagon has just come to a halt—and I'm going out to get drunk.

Nat

168

■■■■■■■■■■■■■

POSTSCRIPT

■■■■■■■■■■■■■

■■■■■■■■■■■■■

In august of 1962 it was announced that a number of the executives of 20th Century-Fox were resigning or retiring from active service with the company. Among these was one who has appeared prominently in the Papers, Joseph H. Moskowitz. Peter G. Levathes stepped down as executive in charge of production in favor of Richard Zanuck, the son of the new president, Darryl F. Zanuck, and a film producer in his own right. Subsequently, Levathes, after an interlude in the company's television activities, left altogether. W. C. Michel had already announced his departure from active service during the course of the pages that occupy this volume, but he remains a member of the company's board of directors.

Other men who have figured in the Papers and who had participated closely in the production of Cleopatra, like Sid Rogell and Doc Merman, likewise left the company.

During the autumn of 1962, Darryl F. Zanuck, having completed post-production work on his own film, The Longest Day, which opened to excellent reviews and prosperous business at the Warner Theater, New York, on October 4, became the working president of 20th Century-Fox. Maintaining that it was his responsibility as president to decide what should stay in or go out of the final version of Cleopatra, he terminated Joseph Mankiewicz's association with the picture after differences in Paris, where the director came to show his cut of the picture to Zanuck. Mankiewicz, noted as a bad man to tangle with verbally, had a few things to say.

Back in New York, in order to state his position, Zanuck summoned a full-dress press conference in the new boardroom that the new management at 20th Century-Fox had created out of what had been Spyros Skouras' office. Skouras, now chairman of the board, found quarters in what had been the old boardroom, just a few steps from the elevators.

To refute Zanuck, who had stressed that duty demanded he take over from Mankiewicz, the latter, upon his return to New York, called a press conference of his own in the sedately elegant town house he occupies on the upper East Side of the city. He sadly acknowledged that he was indeed "off the picture." "I've been a cotton-picker too long [in the Hollywood fields] not to know that Old Marse can do with the cotton exactly what he wants," he stated. According to the New York Herald Tribune, when Mankiewicz was later asked to participate in a TV program, "The World of Darryl F. Zanuck," he replied that he would do so, but only if the title were changed to "Stop the World of Darryl F. Zanuck."

Charles Einfeld withdrew from his position as vice-president in charge of advertising, publicity, and exploitation at the end of 1962, and ceased to be employed on a full-time basis by 20th Century-Fox.

By the winter of 1962, Elizabeth Taylor had completed a family holiday in Switzerland and had rejoined Richard Burton—this time in London—to make another film together, but for a different studio. During the filming of The VIP's, Miss Taylor and Burton resided in separate suites at London's Dorchester Hotel.

By now two salutary things had happened to Joseph L. Mankiewicz. One, he had married Rosemary Matthews, who had been, it will be recalled, a production assistant on the film. The other, he enjoyed a rapprochement with Darryl F. Zanuck, and the two went off to Spain in happy agreement that new battle sequences were needed to replace some of the hasty work done toward the end of production back in the summer of 1962. The principal actors did not participate, though a few hours' work was performed by them in London, which rounded out the circle that had begun for Cleopatra there in 1960.

The initial advertising placed to herald Cleopatra's opening contained an unusual device for attention: neither the title of the film nor the names of any of the people associated with the film were used. With the name of the theater and the price scale ($5.50 top) only a painting of Miss Taylor and Burton as Cleopatra and Antony was employed. Newsweek quoted an observation to the effect that, as Zanuck could not put his own name on the picture, he left everybody else's off.

This mode of advertising made Rex Harrison, not represented in the painting as Caesar, the forgotten man of the cast. The New York Times reported in April 1963 that Harrison, contending his contract had been violated, had brought suit against the film company to obtain "equal billing" with Burton. Harrison meanwhile prepared to re-create his original role for the film version of My Fair Lady, opposite Audrey Hepburn.

It later became Walter Wanger's turn to be the "forgotten man" of Cleopatra. He had not journeyed to Spain with Zanuck and Mankiewicz. On the TV show, "The World of Darryl F. Zanuck," time apparently demanded that Zanuck's career be telescoped in one convenient but rather long jump from The Snake Pit to The Longest Day; yet there was ample time to show the Spain locations for the retakes on Cleopatra, wherein Mankiewicz was clearly the director, Zanuck could be mistaken for the producer, and Wanger was never mentioned. Subsequently it was reported in Variety on April 24 that Wanger had sold out his financial interest to Seven Arts, another film company. Still later, Wanger published a book, My Life with Cleopatra, dealing with his experiences on the project from its inception.

In April, too, a legal separation between Richard and Sybil Burton was announced. No divorce action is contemplated, it was stated, but a huge financial settlement was mentioned. The exclusive story was carried in the New York Mirror of April 4, 1963, in a report by Sheilah Graham.

In May, the first advertising appeared on the second Taylor-Burton film, The VIP's. This time the title was used, but not the names of the stars; only their photograph and the legend: SHE AND HE . . . SEPTEMBER 26. The CBS-TV network took a different tack, however, when it announced a documentary to be shown on October 6 of this year, entitled "Elizabeth Taylor's London."

Meanwhile 20th Century-Fox prepared for its annual meeting of stockholders on May 21. The scene shifted from the traditional setting of the screening room of the company's New York home office to Town Hall, New York, as though to accent a new management. Unprecedented guarantees in the form of cash have come to the company from theater owners all over the world eager to secure Cleopatra in anticipation of the huge attendance it is expected to draw for many years. As a result, the stock-market value of Fox has climbed steadily upward despite the years of losses, including a total of virtually $40,000,000 for 1962 alone. In a notice of the annual meeting mailed to stockholders, it is of interest that "contract settlements with former officers and directors as a group . . . entered into during 1962 aggregated $1,351,200."

At the meeting itself, the gentlemen on the dais trooped on, like an overstuffed Supreme Court, and took their seats five minutes ahead of the appointed time—the elderly men who had survived the changes at Fox mostly to one side of where Zanuck would chair the meeting, the newcomers (except that Skouras was among them) to the other. During those moments, an observer recalling the years of Skouras in command could only find the memory painful as the old man, now part of the supporting cast, blew kisses to the audience and repeatedly waved his hand in the greeting of an undefeated champion.

Then Zanuck, the new star of the show, strode onto the stage to very warming applause. The men at the table stood up. Zanuck signaled for quiet, the gentlemen sat down, and for the next two hours the new president of the new 20th Century-Fox conducted the affairs of the corporation with a businesslike precision punctuated by wit and even by eloquence. Though applause welcomed the announcement that for the first time in many years, the company had shown a sizable profit during the first quarter of 1963, Zanuck was plagued by attacks on many fronts: the cost of Cleopatra and Elizabeth Taylor's compensation; the quality of his associates; the payoffs to executives no longer actively with the company; his own production record of recent years.

If one word seemed to sum up what was most uncomfortable about the session it was "recriminations." Stockholders launched many an assault: "Who is responsible for this ridiculous contract?" (Miss Taylor's) "Return your 50 per cent of the profits of The Longest Day to the company." (To Zanuck) "If a man gets so much for mismanaging, what is a man to get who is successful?" (Of Skouras) Zanuck did his best to satisfy the petitioners, without avoiding or denying claims.

Skouras kept his eyes down during many a challenge, including the moment when a stockholder said, "I am very pleased by the improvement in our president." Zanuck, as though mindful of the embarrassment, quickly acknowledged with "Thank you" and moved on. Queried as to why his son, Dick Zanuck, was a better choice to head production than Peter Levathes, the man he had replaced, Zanuck stated: "Levathes was never in a studio until four years ago. He knows nothing about the motion picture business, or else he'd be here in my shoes today." Pressed to comment on responsibility for the Cleopatra deal, Zanuck said, "The events transpired because there was no central focal head of production—it was split three ways." Indicating that he believed Skouras took more of the blame than he should have, specifically in an article in Newsweek, Zanuck would only state that "I do not absolve Mr. Skouras of his share of the blame."

The ritual the group seemed to demand was that of Khrushchev repudiating Stalin, only in this case with the body still warm. Zanuck remained aloof from any such maneuver, however, and left at least some sentimentalists in the audience with the feeling that he too wished it might not have happened in this way.

And what of the authors? Jack Brodsky resigned from 20th Century-Fox back in October of 1962 to become advertising and publicity director of Filmways, a theatrical and television film company headed by producer Martin Ransohoff, just a short time after his son, Richard Brodsky, was born to Dorothy on September 23 at Mount Sinai Hospital in New York. Nathan Weiss resigned from 20th Century-Fox in January of 1963 to become vice-president in charge of advertising and publicity for an independent film company, Polaris Productions, headed by the producer-director Stanley Kubrick.

Cleopatra had its world première on June 12. Ten thousand onlookers and one hundred policemen were on hand (a Broadway record). The reviews were wildly contradictory. The Herald Tribune (Crist) said, "The mountain of notoriety has produced a mouse." But the Times (Crowther) said, ". . . a surpassing entertainment, one of the great epic films of our day." And the morning after, the box office was in a state of siege.